I'm Just *Charlie*!

THE AUTOBIOGRAPHY OF CHARLIE WARD

Dr Charlie Ward

www.DrCharlieWard.com

First published December 2020

Front Cover: Photograph by Nursel Akifova Feizulova

Back Cover: Photograph by Tony Wilkinson
tonywilkinsonphotography.com

Publisher: Mark Attwood - attwooddigital.com

ISBN: 978-1-8383074-1-7

To My Beautiful Wife
Nursel Akifova Feizulova
&
My Children
Lee, Glenn, Carla and Justin
&
My Grandchildren
Hugo, Alexandro, Baby Lee and Hartley

You Are My Greatest Teachers

— CONTENT —

— PRAISE —

" Charlie has been a big part of my journey in 2020. His gregarious and optimistic outlook on life have kept his followers comforted during this movie of 2020. I have enjoyed our shows together, being able to pick up the phone and just have a chat with him and have a giggle! Super proud of you Charlie! Love Always

— ALPA SONI —

" I've been blessed to know Charlie on a personal level for a short time now and his personality is infectious! Reading his book has helped me realize, that although Charlie's personality is addictive, his book is even more so! I went through every life obstacle and tribulation with him and couldn't put it down. His intimate book of life experiences is exactly, why we all love Charlie so much!

— DAVID NINO RODRIGUEZ —

" A brilliant and bold memoir from a man who visited the depths, of encountering both triumph and tragedy, only to emerge full of light, love, faith, and wisdom. With his signature wit, self-deprecating humour, deep understanding of philosophy and the human mind, Charlie's memoir reminds us all with a little faith and a lot of guts, the best days for humanity truly do lie ahead!

— MELODY KRELL —

“ I can recall the very first time that I came across Charlie Ward on YouTube. It was at the start of the Plandemic Lockdown of 2020, and I was flooding myself with information from podcasts, to interviews, to videos on YouTube to back up this deep knowing that everything was going to be okay. There was a lot of "fear porn" out there, which was completely disempowering. Then there was Charlie. It was a video called "The Two Charlies", and it was an instant intuitive response on my part, where I recognised that this man was all heart.

Fast forward a few months later, and I am suddenly asked on his show for an interview after my new YouTube channel took off - and boy, was I nervous! (I'm never nervous). Before I knew it, he was chatting and laughing with me, just as he does on camera, and all of my anxieties melted away. I realised in that moment, just how genuine Dr. Charlie Ward is. A heart of gold, a man of his word, and a humble human being simply working to shine the light on the truth in order for people to have hope. What you see is what you get. That's it. Simple.

— JC KAY —

"When the Coronavirus first came to light, I said to myself here we go, the Bill Gates apocalypse New World Order is here, everyone around me thought I was nuts! In the search for truth, I stumbled across Charlie Ward on YouTube, I reached out to him and said I can help you with a bit of internet marketing.

A couple of days passed by and my wife caught a glimpse of us both on a live video call. After the call she said: 'That's Charlie Ward' I said: 'How do you know him?' Turns out her best friend and husband know Charlie really well and stay with him in Spain & Dubai. (I never discuss work with her)

What a small world, from there our friendship was set in stone, and I haven't looked back since.

We talk 10+ times a day and it even includes video calls while he's half asleep in bed, or in the bath!

I want to thank Charlie for reinforcing my 5D journey, waking up my family and friends and helping literally millions of people across the world find inner peace. 2020 is a year we will never forget. Where We Go 1 We Go All."

— LEE HEMINGTON —

“ I'm very proud to be trusted by Charlie to publish this autobiography. From the moment I first saw him on his daily walks telling us what an amazing time we are living in, to being inspired by him to start my own YouTube channel, and then appearing on his show, I felt a great resonance with him and knew intuitively he was standing in the frequency of beautiful truth: something I've spent 30 years searching for. In the midst of the craziest year in human history, Charlie has been nothing less than a lighthouse in a Force 10 storm, and his story is remarkable as well as being a bloody good read.

— MARK ATTWOOD —

“ Charlie you have been a beacon of Truth and Light in a world emerging from Darkness. Your success is indicative of your Title "I'm Just Charlie". People love you because you are you! You never give up and you never give in! And Jesus loves you

— TARA DEAN —

“ Charlie is a humble and an honest gentleman who reassures hope and positivity for the future of humanity. It was a privilege to have recorded many videos with him and being a part of the truth movement

— NICHOLAS VENIAMIN —

" Charlie has always been upfront with everybody and very consistent in his story. I like that about Charlie. No hyping, just telling it like it is and what he heard.

He is not our messiah, like he says in just about every video. He is a beacon of hope for a lot of people in these troubling times. Most of all I like him because is still "just Charlie" and he will talk to you personally if needed. That's something not a lot of people do, who have that kind of a following. Keep up the good work! And thanks Charlie for letting me join your shows.

— PETER BIERHOF —

" Charlie Ward was with his videos a Godsend in 2020. To send the truth to a world full of lies. I highly endorse this book to anyone who is a truth seeker. Charlie it is a honour to call you my friend.

— WIM VISSCHER —

" To Everyone reading this and getting to know Charlie like I did I hope like me you find a deeper peace and love for the world and the people in it and the hope and knowing that the world is a wonderful place full of wonderful people and this truly is the best time to be alive. He may not be the messiah but he is a legendary good man living his true purpose and God bless him for the good he brings to the world! We love you Charlie!

— SCOTTY SAW —

" Dr. Charlie Ward is an inspiration to us all during this Revolutionary World War III of Good vs Evil. All that he has endured during his entire life's journey puts him up front & center as a "General Dragon Slayer in the Truther Communications & Podcast arena."

His story is astounding, he is a man of strong moral convictions and a connective force for the millions who hunger for truth & knowledge that "fake news" withholds from the public. God Bless you Charlie Ward.

— SUSAN PRICE —

" Charlie is an absolute blessing on the world! His positivity is infectious, combined with his roguish past, and naughty jokes, it's no surprise that all of us in the truther community find him irresistible. Speaking for myself and the rest of the crew, we are VERY glad to call this true gentleman, a very dear friend. Much Love Charlie!!

— AMELIA LOVE —

" With God, all things are possible! Charlie Ward is a living testament to this. It has been an amazing journey with you thank you for standing for the truth. The BATTLEFIELD is the MIND: GUARD IT!

— FRED NEWELL —

" Charlie and I have known each other for nearly 20 years...we hadn't spoken for at least 10 years and then lockdown happened! Oh boy!!! Did that start a powerful friendship.

We had the science backed facts on the c19 and Charlie had the global financial reboot information. Together our videos climbed from 37 subscriptions to millions. What a time to be alive! Thanks for this wonderful journey together Charlie. Brother from another mother.

— LEE DAWSON —

" If anyone can... Charlie can! What an absolutely phenomenal year it has been! Whilst communities around the World have been tested to the max, driven apart by differing opinions, fear and panic, Charlie Ward has almost single-handedly rounded up people from all over the world together to create an incredible space for the communication of truth.

Charlie, I will forever be grateful to you for encouraging me to speak much more openly, especially around the Children (thanks for getting me banned on FaceAche! Just kidding). Thank you for all you do, you're incredible!

— LUCY DAVIS —

" Charlie is unapologetically truthful. The light he shines is a weapon against evil, as he delivers truth after truth. It has been an honour to be a part of The Charlie Ward Show. He is a conversational genius with a hint of naughtiness and a whole lot of niceness! We love you Charlie!

— CARLY & JULIA —

66 Charlie is a great patriot, truth teller, digital soldier and a guide for many of us during these difficult times... he has enlightened millions of people around world with his reporting... however what I want people to know about Charlie is this... when the cameras are off.. behind the scenes... when no one is watching Charlie is a really good man... a true brother.. never turns his back on a patriot!... that is what I want the world to know! CHARLIE HAS A HEART OF GOLD!

— PRYME MINISTER —

66 I met Charlie back in May of 2020 in the beginning of the plandemic. Many people were in fear of the virus, losing their incomes, the rise of the radical left and so much more. Charlie has brought so much insight and hope to me and all my viewers. I am so thankful to know him and to have done the Remember This Roundtables with him. He is an honorable and respectable man with a great big heart to match his great big smile. May God continue to bless Charlie on his journey, as he has blessed all of us. I love you Charlie.

— DENISE BOLAND —

66 I love Charlie Ward! His dedication to spreading the truth is honorable and well received by his millions of fans. In a world where people had nowhere to go for real intel, Charlie appeared in March 2020 and his YouTube channel grew tremendously. It was just in time for the start of the lockdowns. Charlie provides a sense of relief and calmness to his followers. Thank you, Charlie for all that you do. We love you!

— KELLI RIVERS —

> " we not me

> " Thank you Charlie for being a voice of encouragement during these crazy times of disinformation and fear-mongering! And thank you for opening your platform for so many to share their views that are ignored and squashed by the social media and mainstream media. It's so refreshing to have a site where we can openly discuss issues without fear of being censored! Your reassuring smile and hilarious antics have been the perfect antidote to the constant barrage of negativity from the lefties! We love you Charlie!

> " Charlie always encouraged us to listen to our own hearts and in doing so I really began listening to my inner voice. Soon I realized that when NEW Truth was revealed to me - my inner voice had a British accent! And lo' and behold it was Charlie Ward's voice!

So the twats can say whatever they want as I know Jesus loves me when I hear Charlie's voice in my consciousness! Thank you for being such a voice of reason Charlie!

> " The attempted destruction and division of mankind, actually resulted in a global unification and coming together of people who would not have otherwise connected. I think Charlie created more of those connections than anyone else. It's not a coincidence I was one of them, and I'm grateful.

—

" Charlie what an adventure it's been on this journey talking the NUMBERS together! And getting to know you as a good friend. My YouTube channel "PSYCH CLUB" only really took off after being on your show, so again ThanQ...Even the title of your book I'M (22) JUST (70) = 92 (Numbers) CHARLIE (56) = 148 (Donald J. Trump) shows the Numbers!

Looking forward to many more wonderful times & years through the "Trump Millennium" with you Charlie!

— TOM SIDNEY BUSHNELL —

" The Best is Yet To Come!

— ANIA KONIECZEK —

" Thank you for offering me the opportunity to introduce the heyoka to the world Charlie Ward and enabling me to begin work on fulfilling my life mission - ending mental illness slavery on planet earth - and for that may we all be truly grateful!! God Bless you Charlie Ward.

— DAVID IAN ROGERS —

" It is in our darkest moments we must focus to see the light, and it is then our gift to others to help them see it too. This is what Charlie Ward does daily for millions

— LIZ BLISS —

You only get to see 3% of the world you live in! If I opened the door, to show you what the other 97% looked like, you would go into shock, similar to an explosion!

Because you are misled, you are misinformed. You are lied to!

My book is opening that door, to the 97%, page by page. I would advise you not to dive in and read it all at once…just go step by step and absorb each chapter. You will experience many emotions. Anger because you were betrayed, sorrow from being denied what was rightfully yours as a human being, resentment of those you trusted and also happiness, in knowing you have free will, to live your life, the way you want to live it. A plethora of emotions, not just now, tomorrow or even next week or next month but for the rest of your life. You will look back and be glad that you had the courage, to open the door of 'truth' and look at the devil, to realise how *small* the evil was, who made you believe otherwise.

If someone offered you £1,000,000 to write your life story…what would your answer be?

Well, I was offered this opportunity 10 years ago, by Max Clifford and I turned it down!

I believe there is always a 'right' time to do something in life, no matter what the circumstances are. Do you know what I mean? That 'gut' feeling. I now know that I made the right choice a decade ago, when I turned down that offer because it would not be what this book is today. And you will see clearly why, as you go along.

This is my truth and my memories…no one else's!

It's not another person's perception of me, it's from me.

It's not just who I mingled with, it's from me.

It's not for a limited audience, it's from me.

It's not cashing in on fame, it's from me.

From me to you. That's it!

Yes, it's that simple. It's my personal life story, just as I see it and have lived through it.

It certainly has been a fulfilling journey, of extreme highs and deeply tragic lows. And it all began, with my arrival into this world, on 8th June 1960.

So get comfortable and join me, in taking a trip down memory lane and into the nooks and crannies of my 60 years! Six decades of people, places and many, many experiences!

— CHAPTER 1 —
FOUNDATIONS *OF* CHILDHOOD

8TH JUNE 1960

I was the first-born son of Richard Norman Ward & Joan Mildred Ward and within a year, the family expanded and I was joined by my brother with an additional three sisters in three consecutive years.

Benjamin James was born in June 1961.

Philippa Mildred was born in 1962.

Priscilla Ruth was born in 1963.

Rachel Pauline was born in 1964.

My mother had five children in five years.

My earliest memory is when I was 4 years old and I was taken to Anglesea Road Hospital in Ipswich, with pneumonia. I remember my mother coming to visit me and she brought me a big glass bottle of Lucozade, which was covered in a yellow clear cellophane and I loved the fizzy bubbles and orange flavour! Those people of my age will remember this. Another clear memory during my stay in hospital was when my mother brought in three wooden shelves! She had brought them along with her, so that I could help her cover them in a gingham Fablon which is a sticky back plastic. These were going to be put up in our newly refurbished larder.

We were living at 84 Onehouse Road in Stowmarket. We always lived in detached houses, so to be detached from other people who were not of the same faith and you would probably have said that our family was 'middle class' back then. We appeared normal from the outside, except for no television aerials or radio aerials on the rooftops, as television sets were not allowed in our religion. They regarded them as a 'pipeline of filth' into the house and nowadays, I wonder if they may have been right! Over the years we moved to 34 Temple Road and further down the line we moved house, to 91 Lockington Crescent.

As young kids, we got on pretty well together and we always stuck together as a team. It was pretty old fashioned, as me and my brother had household chores, like clearing out the rubbish and looking after the chickens, etc. and my sisters would keep the house clean and tidy and did all the jobs that girls generally were told to do in the house. I remember growing up with lots of different people looking after us as children, from older teenagers to young women, this was because my father owned his own business and my mother unfortunately, had so much ill health and was admitted to various hospitals throughout our childhood and we needed looking after. I never felt particularly comfortable with this situation as a young lad, as there were just lots of females coming in and out of our house and being around us all the time. There were things that happened that you can't describe or even put into words to explain how you feel but I just had to accept everything as it was, and if you don't talk about things, they become 'normal'.

As a young boy, I was very energetic and full of life!

I wanted to do so much but was not allowed to and I felt so restricted by my parents' belief and faith in the Plymouth Brethren, they had so many rules to obey with so many limitations. I felt isolated and detached from others, especially in school. At my first school, Combs Ford Primary School in Stowmarket, we were not allowed to participate in any types of sports or games and we were not allowed to attend school assembly. So we would have to wait outside in the corridor, bored, until assembly was over, then we would go to our lessons. My parents ordered us as children, to avoid playing or conversing with other children, unless of course, the children came from the same religion. Each weekday, we'd get escorted to school, picked up at lunchtime and taken home to eat our food with our family, then return to school to continue our lessons and at the end of the day, they would come and pick us up to go home. And the reason we ate our lunch at home and not with other children is because they believed in separation from 'evil'. We weren't allowed to mix or eat with anyone, who was deemed 'lesser' than them, as they regarded themselves as the 'Elite', the Chosen Ones. You could even question why the 'elders,' would put us into school in the first place if they were the 'elite'! But they didn't have their own schools in those days but I do believe things have changed now and they have their own schools now.

My mother used to say to me "School's not important, school's irrelevant, it's just a process…'The Rapture's', (which meant, the end of the world is coming!) so you don't need to worry about school."

This even included things like my teeth! I remember it all, like it was yesterday, I was sent to the school dentist who filled my mouth with fillings but I never needed my teeth fixing! I was just told not to worry about it, the Rapture's coming! I only found out later in life, that the work they did on my teeth was barbaric and unnecessary. When I had my fillings removed and replaced, I found out how unnecessary they were. But back in those days, some dentists just did the work to get paid by the government, to make their business worthwhile.

Me, my brother and sisters were constantly being told the same thing, over and over, the Rapture is coming!

And we were assured, this would happen before the year 2000. My Cousin Mark, worked for his father's company called 'Bradleys' and he even had a bet with a co-worker, Mr. Proctor "I bet you one pound that we are not here in the year 2000". Mr. Proctor told him that he was completely mad, he would certainly take the bet on. Sadly, Mr Proctor died before the year 2000, so he never had the chance to claim his winnings.

If I ever questioned my parents about other religions, they would reply that "Many are called but few are chosen, as we are The Chosen Ones."

We didn't have many celebrations in our life. There were no Easter, no Christmas, no Birthday recognition, no gifts, no exchanges, no treats, and no nothing. Maybe because of having so much restriction, I was always fascinated by things, it was in my personality. Just seeing kids enjoying

Christmas and Easter and Birthdays, it appealed to my adventurous side, things needed to be explored! And I was the perfect person to do this.

Another funny memory was, when I was eating my dinner with the family and my uncle and auntie came to visit us, about half way through our meal my brother James said "Daddy, they are nowhere near as bad as you said they were!" This stuck with me because of how embarrassed my father was and it taught me that just because others say something about another person, it doesn't make it true.

With all of these restrictions in my life, I wanted to be in control of my own money and to make my own pocket money, so I decided when I was twelve years old, to go and get a job doing a paper round. I ended up doing three paper rounds in total, Monday to Friday. I would be at the shop by 6am in the morning, I would deliver the papers through the streets of Combs Ford in Stowmarket and I would finish my rounds at 8am. Then I'd rush home and have some breakfast, get dressed and get straight to school, five days a week. Over the years, I masterminded another way to get further income from the newspapers. Each Friday after school, I would go back to those houses that I had previously delivered to and knock on each door to see if I could get the papers back from them. I would put them in my bag and the rest went on the trailer that was attached to the back of my bike, I would take them home and store them in the coal shed. Then, each month my father would find someone with a van so I could return the papers to the 'pulp department', at the East Anglian Daily Times paper mill in Ipswich. They would give me money for the papers that I returned and when I wanted even more money, I would go round other people's paper rounds and collect their newspapers as well! That was the business part of me, which was certainly passed down from my father. I loved having the freedom of my own money and it felt so good to be able to buy my own things, even if they got confiscated from me by my mother! Who always regarded sports as 'filth and unnecessary! (This was her indoctrination and not her true feelings.) But this didn't deter me from liking Ipswich Town Football Club and my heroes in those days were the captain Mick Mills, Trevor Whymark (who was a neighbour in Onehouse near my Uncle's farm), Kevin Beattie, Arnold Muhren and Frans Thijssen from Holland. (These were the first two foreign footballers in the

UK bought, by Bobby Robson.) I would buy a scarf as a treat, with my hard-earned money but I could guarantee within 24 hours, it would disappear! I didn't know where my scarves had vanished too, until a couple of years later when I was being nosey in my mum's bedroom and when I looked under the bed, I was stunned to see that between the bed and the mattress, were all of my scarves! My mum had been stealing them!

My dear mother was put down as having mental health issues and she was regularly admitted into general and mental hospitals for most of our lives. One time, she had an appointment for the electric shock treatment, this was intended to clear her mind of the demons inside of her thoughts. But when she came back home, she didn't even recognise her own family! It was so sad to watch her like this because now I know that she clearly wanted to be heard and no one was listening to her, supporting her and could not even understand her. She wanted to be free from the constraints of this religion and she never found the courage to leave. So, she chose to detach herself instead from her existence, with Johnny Walker Red Label whisky. She was clearly an alcoholic and combined with the concoction of drugs that she was taking for her mental state, you can imagine what it was doing to her mind, body and soul.

Strangely enough, in our religion, at the age of 12, the elders and my own father would encourage us to drink whisky, it was a masculine thing to do, a coming of age so you're old enough to drink and it was almost like an initiation. But this was done at home or in other homes of the 'Peebs', it's a nickname for the Plymouth Brethren people. Yes, I was part of the naughty boys that enjoyed drinking and plenty of it!

Maybe my mum had the same initiation when she was aged 12 and it just evolved from there?

My mother told me a story about her favourite cousin one day, whom she missed so very much and still wished she had contact with him. They were very close when they were growing up in the Brethren. She talked so much about him. His name was David Hemery and he was a former track and field athlete who won 'Gold' at the Mexico Olympics in 1968 for the 440 yard high hurdles which is now called the 400 metre hurdles. She told me that he left the religion the year before I was born, so that he could compete for the Olympics as the religion did not want him to compete, so the only option was to break free for something that he loved doing. We did see him on a few occasions on the coast of Essex and Suffolk hurdling over the breakwaters! Running off sand with the barnacles on the breakwaters, which can be razor-sharp if you brush past them. This is why he obviously never hit a hurdle and this must have enhanced his abilities. In later years, I reconnected with David and asked him if all that my mother had told me about him was true…he said yes. That did make me smile, it gave me a really warm feeling inside.

You may ask, "Where was your father, when all of this was happening to your mother?"

Well, he was so busy with his shoe shop business and he was also paying a lot of attention to the other women that were looking after us, when we were children and during the times when my mother was ill. You could just sense it, that he was just a little bit too over-friendly with them and I didn't feel comfortable with my father acting like this with them. The females would stop overnight in the spare room, in our detached house and I used to find it very unusual that he would go and to settle them down for the night, like he was saying goodnight and tucking them in, similar to what he did with his own children. But something felt 'perverted' and not quite right, it always made me feel uncomfortable that my father was doing this to the other women.

Interestingly, when my mother died, my father landed up marrying one of the girls who was originally one of his helpers, who also was called Joan.

My father was hard-working and honest as a businessman and deeply devoted to his religion. He would tell me to look in the mirror every morning when I woke up and repeat these words…"Oh, wretched man that I am." It certainly was not a positive affirmation to oneself!

Punishment came in three levels. The first level would be a simple telling off if I had disagreed with what he had said and he would send me to my bedroom. The second level, would be a smack on my bottom and this would be if I had done something really naughty and disobeyed them. The third level, would be the ultimate shaming experience, I would have to confess, not just to my father but elders (or priests as they called them) and to all of the other people in the church and tell them every single detail of what I did and why I did it. Now, this may sound silly but it was the way that they asked you the questions. For example, I got caught buying a book called 'Health & Efficiency'. It was a book with lots of pictures of nudity in and maybe you would say it was an old fashioned style of pornography, as it had naughty pictures in but that's why I bought it! And I was caught with this book red-handed, I was having to describe, in detail, why I wanted to buy the book? How I felt looking at the pictures in the book? Did the book stir any feelings in me? But doing this in public didn't sit right with me and looking back, I would call this perverse as I was only a young boy.

Dead opposite to our house, is where my uncle Fergus lived and I would spend times there playing games with my cousin. On occasions when I was visiting the house, my uncle would say discreetly to me and away from anyone else "I need to inspect your private parts, just to make sure that they are healthy." He'd have me drop my trousers, so I would get out my 'willy' just so that he could look at it, to see if it looked healthy. As he was looking at it and playing with it, he would explain how to make my penis go hard. He told me not to tell anyone, I was 10 years old, I was only a child. I never ever told anyone about this, I kept it a secret until many years later when my cousin Adrian told me that this man did the same thing to him. So, I can only imagine he did it to a number of other children too.

With all of this internal conflict going on inside of me and now entering new territory of the Combs Ford Middle School, my personality went from good boy to naughty boy pretty quickly! Well, it had to start sooner or later didn't it! And this is where it began…My parents sent me to stay with the Jackson family one time and they lived in Retford, Nottinghamshire. It was not unusual for the Brethren to stay amongst their own people from other villages, towns and cities. Whilst staying a short time with them, I was busy playing in their garden and wondered what it would be like to start a small fire that I could stamp out. So, I sneaked into their woodshed to start the fire but it became bigger and bigger and I couldn't put the flames out! I managed to burn the whole shed down and I was sent home and punished!

I was becoming a rebel in a very short space of time at school, I went from zero to hero! I was given the opportunity one morning by one of the naughty boys, 'Tank' but his real name was Neil Prentice. His catapult had been confiscated and put in the headmaster's office for safe-keeping. Before assembly, he told me "If you want to be in our gang, you have to go into the headmaster's office and get my catapult back and I'll give you a pound for it." I thought quickly "What shall I do? I always love having money and being part of a gang might be fun." I couldn't refuse! "Yes, I'll do it!" So, when assembly started, I left the corridor and headed towards the headmaster's office. I opened the door, looked around the room and began to search for Tank's catapult. Yep, I found it! Along with plenty of other items too! So, I took all of the items and put them into my locker and I ended up giving Tank his catapult back and took a pound for it and then there was Carl Jones, he had a peashooter and I got another pound for that! And then I ended up selling all of the other confiscated items back to their rightful owners for £1 each too! But then the headmaster caught me and punished me for breaking into his office and then I got the cane. When I got home, my parents then smacked me for getting a caning at school! Well, that was normal in those days.

This is where I got my first ever girlfriend and her name was Janet Driver.

Janet was someone who remembered me from primary school and she felt very sorry for me because she remembered me getting bullied and having beatings and being picked on all the time in the other school because I was different, from the rules of our religion and being disconnected from other children. The kids would talk about television, radio, sports, take away meals, songs, holidays, birthday's and it went on and on, I had no idea what they were talking about! And now because of my 'new' naughty behaviour, she asked me if I wanted to go out with her.

I said, "Yes! Where to?"

She said "No, I just wanna go out with you"

I said "Yeah, but where to?" (I had no idea what she meant)

She said again "No, I just wanna go out with you"

I said "Yeah, but where?"

Then somebody explained to me that she wanted to date me! So, we became boyfriend and girlfriend and I used to ride my bike to her house. Janet lived about 10 miles away from me, in a place called Mendlesham. I couldn't believe that I'd attracted Janet, just because I had been naughty! It seemed that being a 'good' boy who's not allowed to do anything and felt no use to anyone, was slowly dissolving away. This way was way a lot more fun!

During this time my father decided I needed a hobby, the year was 1972.

My first ever lesson in business. My father thought it would be a good idea to give me some chickens! So, he purchased six, day-old chickens that cost 27p each. But within a short time, I found out that I could get chickens for 5p each, from another farmer. So, I bought loads of em! Believing I'd found a better deal but the trouble these ones turned out to be cockerels and they didn't lay eggs! That's why they were cheaper and so I learned a lesson that my dad knew what was best in business. I did mention to you that my brother and I were in charge of the chickens over the years. We started with the six chickens and ended up with having thousands of them over many years. When the chickens grew bigger we used to keep them at my Uncle Esmonds farm, in one of his old Nissan huts from the Second World War in Glebe Farm in Onehouse. We supplied a large number of eggs to the people of Stowmarket. There were times when I was ruthless in business, if the chickens weren't making enough money from the sale of the eggs, then they didn't get any chicken meal food. What we did instead was to put them out in the field just to eat grass. In those days we thought that was a cheap way of doing things and it turns out, this was the best way to feed them. The eggs improved in quality and it ended up better all round, with better quality eggs and less cost to us, in the long run. The natural grass was so much better than the feed. We used Rhode Island chickens crossed with Light Sussex. Rhode Island gave you the quality of the egg and Light Sussex gave you the size, so it turned out a good quality large sized egg and we would use grit to make the eggshell nice and strong. I did have good fun on the farm.

Then one day, Janet Driver finished with me but not because of the chickens.

She ended our relationship because she caught me with another girl or two. I did not think back in those days about repercussions and consequences, I just did things for fun! Looking back though, I did betray her but she did give me a good telling off for my naughtiness and she told me, that the other girls were her friends and then she went home crying but I must confess that the naughtiness was appealing to me and with all of the rules that I always had to obey, naughty was more exciting! It was like an adrenaline rush with these girls suddenly wanting to be my friend because of my rebellion, like breaking into the headmaster's office. It was so lovely to have so much attention from everybody because in my childhood, nobody wanted to have anything to do with me. I was so detached from the children and this felt endearing, that they all wanted to be my friend. Then I began to play even naughtier! And I did, with the Eton twins, Wendy and Carol. I decided to go out with them both at the same time! We would kiss and hold hands but it was challenging trying to keep them apart, as I did not want one twin telling the other twin about me. They didn't know they had the same boyfriend! Those were fun days!

I was getting more confident and so, I went against my parents' wishes and visited a Chinese takeaway, which we were told not to go into one of these places because they were different from us. The Chinese family lived next door to us, the first 'foreign' family to move into our small town of Stowmarket. My father said "You don't talk to them because they are different to us." My father's religion referred to them as the 'communists' next door. Well, I had my own pocket money and these Chinese people owned the take-away shop, so I decided to go in there one day and get some egg fried rice, I thought "It can't be that bad, can it?" I tasted it and it was really, really nice and at the same time, I was thinking "Why can't we talk to these people? They make really good food!"

My life continued like this for a few more years, until one day, I finally had enough of them all and I made my decision to run away from home, to see what else was out there, in the real world!

My mum, Joan Ward

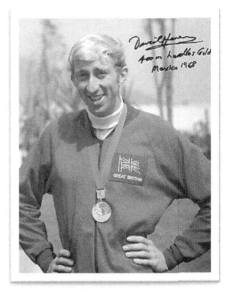

David Hemery

Angelsea Road Hospital

— CHAPTER 2 —
WARDS OF STOWMARKET

As soon as I finished school, at the age of 16, I was learning my father's trade in shoes. This was because I was the eldest son and the next in line, to continue the family business, Wards of Stowmarket. My great grandfather was Frank Ward and the company passed down to my grandfather, Norman Ward and then passed down to my father. He was a well-known and highly respected man in those days and was a very hard working person. The shop was open Monday to Friday with general opening times. Saturday and Sunday was for family unity and the Brethren. One of my Uncle's, Frank Harvey Ward (Known as Uncle Harvey), had a shoe repair business at the back of this shop and they worked together as a great team. Adjacent to Wards of Stowmarket shoes, was our clothing company store, Norman Wards and these were all managed by family and trusted members of staff. I remember Mrs Plumb who ran the daily business of the shoe shop, as she was the manager beneath my father. There was one particular staff member that probably understood me the most, her name was Veronica Mumford. She was always very kind to me and considerate, as we worked together in the shop and not because I was the son of the owner, but because of who I was as a person. I felt like she could see my oppression, from the religion. Her husband is ingrained in my memory, as he was a millionaire and I found out from Veronica that he could not read nor write but had lots of common sense. This stood me in good stead for many, many years.

After about six months, I was already getting fed up working in the shop, it was doing my head in! Do you know that women and men as customers are very different in their shopping behaviour and ways of purchasing goods? Women could try on ten pairs of shoes, look at a variety of handbags in one hour and then proceed to walk out of the shop, without spending a penny! This made no sense to me. Men would enter the shop, try on a few pairs of shoes and purchase something. Our shoe store had three departments, the men's department, the women's department and children's department. The ladies department was my least favourite to work on and the only bonus for me, was that I got to spend time with some very attractive women but I did not always enjoy kneeling at their feet, especially when they left without buying anything, after I had given them all of my attention! Some feet did not always smell pleasant too! But that was part of the job. During this time, I gained experience in the construction of a shoe and learning how a shoe is manufactured in the industry, where it came from and how each individual shoe is made. This was key information, so that when I was dealing with our customers, I would know what to suggest to them, as I listened to their requirements. Many of the people who came into the shop were extremely wealthy, so it was important for my father to give me a lot of knowledge and experience.

One particular client was the Duke of Norfolk, he was someone I distinctly remember because he had size 14 feet! When he visited our shop, he would buy up to five pairs of shoes, at a time. Now, this is what made sense to me, that when you visit a shop, you actually purchase an item. So, when Norfolk decided on the shoes he wanted to purchase from the shop, we would get the order and use his 'lasts' (pronounced as lahsts). This is a model of your feet that is made from wood, so that you can make the shoe around them. Some of Norfolk's shoes would be handmade by my father's cobbler and some would then be sent to the shoemaker, such as Loakes or Barkers and made around the 'lasts'.

I remember Clarks shoes head office in Street, Somerset, where they also owned the Bear Inn Hotel. In this hotel, I remember it really well because there was no bar to have a drink in because their religion did not consume alcohol but our religion did. My father had sent me over to Barkers of Earls Barton and Clarks of Street, as an apprentice, where I stayed with other families from the Brethren.

Did you know that the shoe trade is deeply religious?

Clarks Shoes were Quakers (Lance Clark)

Barrett Shoes is Jewish (Arnold Ziff).

"K" Shoes (Spencer Crookenden)

Barkers (William Barker and Eric Ward)

Loakes are also religious.

They all knew each other and had a lot of respect for each other and they were extremely honourable men in the shoe trade, which is a rare trait nowadays.

As I was in the Brethren, I was told that my wages would be higher than other staff members that were outside of the religion, it could even be as much as 50-100%. This sounded appealing, but it also made it very difficult to leave the job financially but it did give me the opportunity, to save money of my own. Here I was, sixteen years of age and very restless. I wanted to leave the shop and not work with my father, and I was also fed up living at home, with my parents. Because of how bored and restless I was, they wondered if working for my Uncle Esmond in Bradleys, may be a better option. So I did, and for a period of time, I managed to save enough money to leave home, I gathered about £100 into savings. My plan was to run away and I was getting ready to make my move. It was 1976.

My aim was to get to the Ideal Home Exhibition in London! I know, you must think that's not the first greatest adventure for someone, but it was for me! I was intrigued to know what it was all about, as I had heard all about the event from people, so I wanted to see it for myself. Even the name of it appealed to me! "What's it all about?" I used to think. So, I got the train from Stowmarket to Liverpool Street London, then from Liverpool Street, I took the Underground to Earl's Court and then onto the Ideal Home Exhibition. I thoroughly enjoyed the experience! And when my time was coming to an end at this exhibition, as I had already made the decision to run away from home, I followed my next idea. I left

London and got the train to Dover, where I got a lift from a lorry driver, who was going to travel from France, into Spain. This was perfect! He dropped me off in Zaragoza, Northern Spain. I was having an amazing time! As you can imagine though, with only £100 in my wallet, lots of travelling, eating, drinking and not working, I ran out of money after three days! So, even though I had run away from home, I ended up phoning my mum up!

She asked me where I was and I said "Don't worry about where I am, I will get home somehow." My only option was to hitchhike because back in those days, you could easily get a ride. I got another lorry driver to give me a lift, which brought me back up through France and when he came to England he said "Where do you want me to drop you off?" I said "I don't know." He ended up dropping me off at Chorley Service Station, which is not even close to my home! I then telephoned my mum again and said "I'm at Chorley Service Station, can you come and get me?" It seemed like running away from home did not really work out for me! I had to wait about twelve hours, for my mum to find someone to pick me up and bring me back home. My parents were both relieved that I was safe and back home with them again, thankfully I was not punished! As they were just pleased to see me alive. In my mother's own way, she understood me. I can see that now because she wanted to escape too, that was probably why she never punished me. My dad couldn't understand what I did or why I did it. He was always so polite in his response to things, as he did not like to upset people but my mum was always upsetting people!

I got a surprise not too long after this experience! My father told me that he was going to put me on a short course, so I could get my driving license. I had been driving since I was 14 years of age, my father had purchased a Fiat 500 variomatic from a lady from Poland called Mrs Snuckowski. I used to drive in an airfield and on some farms, which gave me lots of practise. My official driving lessons began just one month before my test, every other day I was enhancing my skills, on the correct manoeuvres and rules of the road. My test was booked for 8th June 1977 at 9am and I passed my test, the first time around! This was not meaningful just because I had passed my test, it was also my 17th birthday and previously none of my birthdays, had ever been important. Now suddenly, this time around, it was an occasion where I had given myself a treat! And it made me feel good inside, with pleasant satisfaction. Sadly, the examiner kept my lesson going on for another hour, even after passing my test! Because he said "The last time I passed a person that was as cocky as you, he killed himself on the way home!" With this stern statement "You are NOT to remove your L plates until you arrive safely back home." I loved being able to drive myself around, it gave me much more independence, as I could take myself to different places. The one place I was unable to drive to, was church. This was because my father had a Peugeot 504 estate car, which had three rows of seats inside, which fitted all of us comfortably together, as a family unit. I would like to point out some of the positive elements of our religion, namely Fellowship. Attending our church was a daily experience.

Monday	Prayer Meeting 7pm Stowmarket (Milton Road)
Tuesday	Prophetic Word 7.45pm Ipswich (Cauldwell Hall Road)
Wednesday	Reading 7.45pm Ipswich (Cauldwell Hall Road)
Thursday	Interchange Reading 7.45pm (Aldeburgh or Colchester)
Friday	Local Reading 7.45pm Stowmarket (Milton Road)
Saturday	9-10am (Once a month 6-7am Care Meeting) (Cauldwell Hall Road)
Sunday	6-7am Breaking of bread - 9-10am Reading Ipswich - 1-2pm + 5-6pm Preaching

Because Sunday was a full day in church, we would entertain people in our house and visit other families. There would be chatting, children playing together and refreshments for everyone. There were different types of entertainment, I would play my guitar! We would often be invited to other houses, as my sister and myself would sing and play the instruments and we did sound good together. We memorised the songs that the Brethren believed to be, the 'right' music to listen to, but I found other ways to cheat! We played cassette tapes and learned how to follow the music, lyrics, timing, etc. I got into trouble whenever I was caught listening to something that I shouldn't have been playing, it did not deter me from doing it again. Our local meetings were held at Stowmarket and the men of the Brethren lead the services. Women were allowed to choose a hymn for the beginning and end of a meeting, by saying the number of the song that they had chosen. I do remember that I was happy to go to service, just not every single day of the week! I loved listening to the hymns and the singing voices, it sounded so nice. When we attended the larger gatherings, the choir sounded the best of all. I still love choir music to this day, it brings me such peace listening to the Welsh Male Voice Choir and other beautiful vocals.

We had monthly meetings that were held for the whole of the Plymouth Brethren religion. This was based in Bath Road, Bristol and families would travel far and wide around the British Isles and Europe to gather together for union. We would travel there by coach, all the way from Ipswich. This took us about seven hours to arrive but it was worth it for me, as now I had become more interested in the girls! It was a great opportunity to 'technically' date someone. I only attended those monthly meetings because it widened my horizons, to the different girls that travelled far and wide. So, prior to these meetings, it was quite important for me to be on my best behaviour and aim to do all the right things at home, so I would not be punished. Naturally this gave me the opportunity of exploring further with the females and seeing what was in it for me!

That was when I got lucky and met Lucy Labett! She was the best looking girl that everyone wanted to date and she chose me to go out with.

My Grandfather's shop, Norman Ward

My Great Grandfather's shop, Frank Ward

Wards of Stowmarket Childrens Department

Fiat 500 Variomatic

— CHAPTER 3 —
BOY *TO* MAN

The first time I met Lucy, my friend and many other lads, thought she was the best looking girl on the market! My mate was trying to get a date with her but I beat him to it! I think she was attracted to my naughty boy side but we certainly did have some chemistry between us. You know that feeling, when you can't explain something or put it into words and the physical reaction is magnetic? Well, that's what happened with us two. I felt that I had done rather well, with Lucy as my girlfriend and after we had dated for some months, I was told by her father that it was time that I got married to Lucy. My response was "I can't afford to get married" but that was not really the full story, I was actually having internal trauma! He added "Well, we need to boost the numbers on the Isle of Wight (to expand the Brethren community) so, if you move to the Isle of Wight from Ipswich, I'll buy you a house as a wedding present, I'll furnish the house throughout and I will give you a job with twice the salary, than you are earning now and I will provide you with a vehicle too." As I wanted to leave the grips of my parents, the religion and their control over me, so the option of leaving Ipswich to live with Lucy, was an extremely attractive offer and it seemed, at that time, the better option and the lesser of the two evils. As you can probably see, there was an element of an arranged marriage and it was cleverly done.

Well, as a young man, this all sounds like a bloody good idea! I'd be completely set up! So, after one year of dating, we got married at the Plymouth Brethren Church on London Road in Waterlooville near Portsmouth, this was only because this was the only church that would give us a license for marriage, as the Isle of Wight could not offer us, the license of unity back then. It was a very informal ceremony, as we arrived at the church wearing normal but smart clothing, for our wedding. For some reason within our religion, men never wore ties around their necks and I still don't know why? There was no explanation for this, it's just how it was. Alan Goody, my best man and friend from Ipswich stood by my side. Sarah Labett, Lucy's sister was her bridesmaid. We then travelled to our new home, which was all set up in Newport on the Isle of Wight.

The first day on my job at The Island Bedding Centre, I was driving proudly to work in my new Sherpa van that had been bought for me by Paul. The Island Bedding Centre supplied furniture and bedding to the hotels on the island and I would work on the shop floor and deliver items that had been ordered.

Now, even though I was a husband with new responsibilities, I still had the kid in me that wanted to explore! Sometimes, I would go out with Lucy's brother Roger Labett, as he would show me around different places on the island. One of those places was a cemetery in Godshill Church in Godshill. Whilst we were walking through the graveyard, we noticed one particular grave that was elevated off the ground and damaged on the corners. It had erosion from over three hundred years, where you could actually see inside this outdoor tomb. The details encrypted on the stone, was of a man in his 90th year and from the 1700's. Well, of course we had to investigate further! We were having fun and just curious, to what we may unearth and we wondered what still may be left inside the grave. Some may call this foolishness but we were young men, who had suddenly become detectives! After we had managed to squeeze through an opening, we found the skeletal remains and I wanted to take the skull home because I suddenly had a great idea! If I could clean it up and put a candle inside of the space, in the skull, it would look eerie but brilliant, all at the same time. I was not intending on resurrecting the dead, just to have a fun lamp in the house. So, I took the skull from its resting place and discreetly carried it home but during the night, I realised what I had done! So many thoughts kept racing through my mind and I decided to put it back where it came from, and no one would ever know. So, I met up with Roger, later that day, with the intention to return the skull to its original resting place but I panicked and threw the half cleaned skull into a hedge in Newport! But obviously, the universe had other plans for me. A man, who was out having a lovely quiet walk with his dog, spotted the skull in the hedge and he phoned the police, who came out immediately 'to the scene of the crime', with a large forensic team. It became local headlines in the Isle of Wight County Press! Saturday, February 17, 1979 'any information about the mystery skull, believed, to be that of a bearded man'…It didn't stop there…it became news throughout the mainstream media and right through the United Kingdom! What had I done?! A massive investigation had taken place to find the killer and the remains of the rest of the body. They reported in the media that they were close to arresting a man, who had murdered the victim. Two scientists had professionally identified the skull as, "it was indeed a man, in his 30's who had been shot through the head, within the past two years, 1977-1979." How was this possible? Were they actual scientific experts in their field? For me, it showed how innocent people can be put into prison, for a crime that they may not have committed. It's also a reminder of how much bullshit we are told, from trusted 'experts' and 'professionals', within their field of expertise.

Roger and I finally had to expose ourselves and tell our families the truth. They said we had to go to the Police station immediately and own up about everything, so we handed ourselves over to the Police and confessed. This was one week later after our shenanigans. The skull was returned to its resting place and the story was never mentioned again, by the local papers or the national news. It must have been embarrassingly palpable for the Police, the Forensics and all the other departments involved. Well, we must have done a great job at cleaning the skull!

Within 10 months of marriage, I became a dad.

My son, Lee Richard Ward was born. The birth was certainly memorable!

Prior to Lee arriving in the world, Lucy had been admitted to St. Mary's Hospital before her delivery date, this was normal procedure back then, for what they call 'observation'. Lucy was 18 years old, the same as myself and she had made a friend whilst she was in hospital, with a 16 year old girl on the ward. Visiting rules only allowed you to go in for one hour only each day. During my visiting hour, I got to know Lucy's friend and her boyfriend, who was 16 years of age. We used to get excited to see our wives during this one hour window and devised a plan between us, so that we could stay longer on the ward than we were actually allowed. When we knew, it was getting time for us to leave, me and this lad would slide under our wives beds! Wait until the coast was clear from the nurses and came back out again, once they'd gone. We just wanted to spend more time with our partners, we had to make the timing spot on, so as not to get caught. There was another lady on the ward, who was super posh. I remember how she kept telling her husband to "iron my dressing gown"! And I even remember the oriental in pattern, isn't it funny how we can remember these little details in life! She did appear to be older in age and her husband was always very precise in following the visiting hour rule. She was not impressed with us dodging the nurses and hiding under the bed but we never got found out or told off!

The baby's due date had arrived and both of our wives went into labour, exactly at the same time! Well, me and this lad had gone into a panic! We were only young and did not have a clue about what to expect, so we joined them in taking laughing gas to see what it did! It certainly helped with the situation even though it was not meant for us dads-to-be but we did have some fun!

For me, having Lee in my arms, my new-born son, I suddenly realised that I had never known what love was, until he came into my life. A baby's love is truly unconditional. At home, I was still working full time but I was a 'hands on dad', I was changing nappies, getting up at night to help Lucy and I just loved spending time with Lee. I enjoyed being a father and was so very proud. There were no problems and life was going well for us.

18 months later, my second son Glenn Ward, arrived in the world.

During Lucy's observation time in hospital, her mother Mary Labett was always there to help her daughter. This was something that I thought highly of in the religion, they were very supportive and families would stick together and look after each other. A stronghold union of the Brethren, helping each other through crisis, times of change, troubles and happiness with an implicit trusted bond. Lois Leary, Lucy's cousin and good friend, was there to support her with her mother. The due date arrived and it was all calmer than the first time around and I did have some more gas but it was for fun, not because I was panicking!

Glenn arrived safely and I had my moment of pride, he was such a beautiful baby.

One time when he was a baby, we were coming back from the church in Portsmouth, going back home to the Isle of Wight, on the ferry. The weather was so bad, that one of the windows broke and his pram was suddenly flooded with cold sea water! He screamed with shock and we couldn't believe that the water didn't drag him away! For the next six months, Glenn couldn't sleep properly, he would keep waking up and crying. When he finally did sleep through, we were so worried that he was sleeping properly!

During Glenn's early life, I decided that I wanted to stop working for my father in law. I had decided to run my own business. Lucy's father asked "What sort of business do you want to do?" I said "I want to be an electrician". I had no idea why I wanted to do electric work or become an electrician. He said "That's fine. I will send you to the Isle of Wight college of Arts and Technology and you can get trained up and qualified". I did know some basics of the subject but he knew I could get a proper trade with a certificate. So he paid for me to enrol in the electrical course, which was part-time. This meant I could still work for him, to earn money alongside the course. He did not want me to leave the Isle of Wight and he did everything in his power, to keep me there.

One year later, I was a Qualified Electrician! Paul Labett knew someone called Ray Lacy, who had a company called Amber Electrics in Newport. I got a job with him as an apprentice, to learn from the best, he was also a lovely person and so, I worked with him on a number of things. He was such a funny man! He kept everything on 'live' which meant that he kept electrocuting himself! As I was still a kid at heart, I found it hilariously funny because I would not work on anything, unless it was turned off but Ray would 'jump' all over the place. His general response would be "Oh shit! I've done it again". But that was just him all over, his personality, he was an adorable person and a great teacher.

The most brilliant job we ever did together, was putting the navigation lights on The Needles, on the Isle of Wight, which are the outermost chalk rocks. It was one heck of a challenging task! There was a tunnel that came from the Forte, which was about 200 meters long and pitch black. This was going to be open to the public. The navigation lights were done in steel wire armoured cable, this was an incredible duty because the cabling alone was incredibly difficult to attach and the Tunnel was wired in a cable known, in the trade, as 'Pyro'. It's a copper pipe, surrounded inside with a powder casing of magnesium oxide, this stops the water from entering the pipe. But you needed that for protection against the environment, so you had to make up all of these joints, which was incredibly difficult to stop the moisture getting in and test every single piece. Then, I had to screw this up to the ceiling, which was damp, cold and dark, with a lamp on my head, whilst doing the job. It was generally windy and wet. I had a tool box, which was by a company called Facom which apparently, was second rated below Snap On, as they were more expensive to buy. Even a screwdriver back in those days could cost anywhere between £25-30 but was guaranteed, quality for life. I did lose some in the sea! But I did find a diver one time, who retrieved it for me! The diver even commented that he had never seen a screwdriver that cost so much money! It was a real big challenge for me but one of those experiences that I will never ever forget.

Carla Jayne Ward, my little girl, came 18 months after Glenn.

It was so lovely to have a little girl in my arms and she looked so sweet.

So here I am, with a wife and three children and I was only, 22 years of age! We had made our home just as we had wanted it, over those years our money was always on 'tap'. This was to keep us there and to keep us happy. But the cracks were getting bigger in our marriage and with my faith in the Plymouth Brethren. I was beginning to feel torn and trapped in my situation.

Sadly, I could not continue to live life within the ties of the religion. There were things happening that went against the grain with me, like, my mother being an alcoholic and everyone around her blaming it on everything else! They put it down to mental health, rather than realising the actual problems that existed. They had this theory that alcohol was "purifying the spirit" but smoking cigarettes was "defiling the spirit" this confused me! Among other things, in this religion and the lifestyle you had to follow.

By this stage of my life, I was starting to question things, "Why is this…?", "Why is that…?" But I was being told, by the others around me, that this is the time, where I now need to have faith, more than ever. But I did not have faith anymore, I had lost it completely. It did not make sense to me and looking back, I was exactly right.

My life began to take on a new and exciting direction.

I had built up a good clientele with my electrical business, on the Isle of Wight, which was simply, through my own hard work. I had one particular client that had an Indian Restaurant in Sandown and without fail, he would call me out on a Friday or Saturday night, something would break down at the restaurant because the electrics were being overstretched! It nearly always ended up, being the thermostat on the cooker. And because I offered an emergency service, for a lot less money, than the South West Electric Board, this led to many call outs to the Indian restaurant, with their weekly problems. I would go out to them, repair the issue at that moment and charge a fair price, then go home.

One day, as the owner was paying me for the work I had just done, he gave me a chicken dish with rice. Well, I thought "No one is going to see me this late at night, so bollocks to it! I'll eat it!" So, I had this curry to eat and then he offered me a beer and I was saying to myself "Oh, that's nice", whilst looking over each shoulder and checking that no one was watching me from behind, because as you know, this was not allowed in my religion.

It was so nice, I really, really enjoyed it. My first ever curry from an Indian takeaway!

And week after week, I would get my emergency call out to this Indian restaurant and enjoy my feast! On this one particular occasion, someone said to me "Charlie, do you want to come out with us tonight, we're going to the boat?"

I said "What's the boat?"

He said "A nightclub"

I said "I've never been to one of them!"

And I thought, "Yeah, I'll come along". I wanted to know what a nightclub was! But I was still dressed in my work clothes and had nothing else to change into, so I just went along with them all, to see what it was all about, this disco place. Now, the Isle of Wight knows everybody and each other and suddenly I was the 'new boy' on the boat! I became the centre of attention with all of the women, which I quite enjoyed! It was very exciting because I had never experienced this before and I didn't quite know what to do but the boys looked after me.

Then they told me "The next time you come to the restaurant, bring some smart clothes to change into and leave the bag in the van". This was so I could change into my clothes after eating my food with them. So, the next time I had the usual emergency call out a week later, I did just as they had suggested. This was becoming more and more regular and I forgot to add in earlier that on a Sunday morning, we had to be in church at 6am. Well, as you can imagine, with the garlic and beer oozing out of my pores and breathe, I was struggling to disguise it and I was getting questioned about my 'scent', whilst still feeling pissed this early in the morning. Yes, it was all a bit of a giveaway!

One time I made a decision, that I could not be bothered to go to church for Sunday service, so I turned off the alarm. By 6.05am, I had the family coming round to the house saying "Where are you?" "Get out of bed!" I said "Leave me alone, I am not feeling well". I was telling the truth, I was not feeling great with all of the booze I had consumed and all of that food, that I had eaten the night before. I was also hoping they would not see any lipstick marks on my cheeks!

My wife was beginning to tell me off and she would say things like, "If they have found out that you've had something to eat in that restaurant, you're in big trouble."

This is where I was beginning to detach from all of them, from Lucy, the kids, my family and her family and everyone, that I had ever grown up with. I was starting to enjoy this new life I'd found and when they turned up another morning, for me to attend church, I simply said "You know what, you can piss off! I don't want to be a part of this, anymore!" They then told Lucy to pack her bags, get the kids things and leave with them, immediately!

They proceeded to take my wife and children from me because of this situation and so, Lucy went home to her family.

My head was all over the place, I was lost. With all of this going on internally and externally, I continued to work hard but my nightly outings became more regular, actually it was every night!

As you can see, I was running away from all of my responsibilities as a husband and a father, I was not dedicated anymore to them and blatantly, irresponsible.

Each time I wished to see my children, "they", being all of my relations, were making things extremely difficult, in different ways. They wanted to be there during my meetings with my children, in case I mislead them, for what they believed to be evil, wrong or untrue. My visits were managed and we had no freedom to just be together alone, as we used to be. On some occasions, my children told me that they were being questioned, after each visit, they were interrogated with things like, "What did he say to you?" "What is he doing?" "Did he do this/that?" etc.

And because of this continual harassment, I made a decision to take this further.

I got a tattoo on my right arm! I chose the design of a love heart with a dagger going straight through it because that was how my heart felt because my whole family rejected me.

I was having regular parties in my house, which was opposite to Martin Nichols' house.

I made sure that on a Saturday night, my parties lasted all night until 6am the next morning, so that the church goers who were setting off for their morning service of prayers, could not miss me or the noise coming from my house! They could see my doors were open and as they walked past me, I ensured to turn up the music! Just to show them that I was having a good time, without them. I felt like putting two fingers up to the establishment of that religion.

During this episode of living on my own, I met a man called Max. I was driving to work one morning when I spotted someone hitchhiking, so I pulled over, stopped the car and he got in the car with me. I can only describe him as looking 'scruffy' and he told me that he lived in a coal shed, I said "What do you mean a coal-shed?"

He told me that he was in a shit position with losing his job, having no money and now he was homeless. I asked him if he would be interested in working for me as a labourer, he turned to me, with a surprised look on his face and said yes! So, I took him to a clothing shop for men 'Top Man' and bought him seven pairs of trousers, seven shirts, ten pairs of underwear, ten pairs of socks, four pairs of shoes and I 'kitted' him out! He even stayed at my house for a few months, whilst I helped him get back on his feet. Max was one of the most honourable, reliable and trustworthy employees that you could ever have wished for, such a smashing young lad. I now know that he owns his own business, has a wife and five children. Synchronicity brought us together and I feel so very proud that I had the privilege of helping him out during his dark times into the light.

'They' would still visit me, asking questions like "Have you managed to sort yourself out yet?" or "Have you got right yet?"

I wanted Lucy to leave the Plymouth Brethren, so that we could live a life that suited us as a family unit. One evening Lucy sneaked round to see me and we had sex on the settee but this was betrayal in the eyes of the Brethren. I proclaimed afterwards "Either you tell them or I will! Because if you tell them, you will be kicked out and if I tell them, you'll be kicked out!" I had set a trap for her. This was the only way I could get her out of the religion and away from them all. Yes, I blackmailed Lucy. The next step was inevitable and her parents kicked her out of the house and she returned to me. It was unpleasant for a time, as our families and other people around us were making our life extremely difficult. Lucy did want our marriage to continue but she was torn emotionally in leaving the religion, her family and all she had ever known.

I got offered an opportunity in timeshare sales in Torquay, Devon. Lucy agreed to leave the Isle of Wight and the Brethren and so, I terminated my electrical business and we moved away from them all, hoping to create a new life in a new place, with a job that sounded amazing!

Alan Goody, best man at my first wedding

The Needle
Isle of Wight

Carla, Glenn and Lee

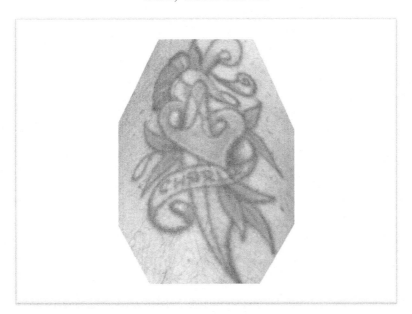

My Tattoo

— CHAPTER 4 —
ESCAPING *THE* CULT

So, we landed in Torquay for our new life together and my job with the holiday clubs in Hillesden Court, Grampian Court and Kingswear Park, based in Devon, UK. This was a modern business concept, which began in the 1960's but was big business for sales in the 1980's, for Britain. The theory was that you had all of the luxury of a lovely apartment, only for the time you needed it, for your own personal use, leisure and pleasure, on the same date annually. The first person that I ever sold a timeshare to, was a police officer that purchased a specific week and he told me this was because he could stay away from all the other police officers during an annual conference! It was at the Imperial Hotel in Torquay and he just wanted to be with his wife and family, in a nice place.

Each timeshare I sold, I was given £1,000 and in my first week I had earned £2,000. Now this made so much sense to me, this was good money!

Within a few short months, both Lucy and I began to realise that we actually had nothing in common albeit the religion and our children. The chemistry had gone and our relationship had no foundation and it crumbled away, which was a very sad period in my life. I thought the world of her and it certainly was a challenge for me to make the decision to end our marriage but I felt clear and certain that I did not wish to be committed to Lucy anymore, as my wife because of all the toxicity connected in different ways, from the past. Lucy did not return to her family for various reasons and remained with the children in Torquay. Divorce was on the cards.

Living on her own with three children and without the support mechanism she was used to having, was incredibly tough for Lucy. She was an amazing woman and as a mother, did such a marvellous job, in bringing them all up, under the circumstances. The environment around her was hostile and difficult, as she was a 'sitting duck' for her family to torment her but she was strong and she managed to pull herself through. Looking back, I should have given much more of myself financially and emotionally but I was irresponsible and not in a good place mentally. I have no excuses and I accept all that I did and did not do but back then, my head was split in two. I did not feel that I knew what was actually going on in my life, I was burying all of these emotions and internal pain, whilst getting drunk. I was still earning money easily but spending it just as easily too, on a lifestyle that was extravagant and I should have been giving Lucy money for being the mother of our children. I was paying her in dribs and drabs and my priority was drinking and partying, I did not realise how my actions, were actually affecting them all. There was immense pressure all around me and when you are used to a support mechanism of beliefs, it is certainly challenging to separate yourself from them. I loved the unity of that religion previously but saw it completely differently, when I was on the other side of it. I had now been disowned and cut off completely from them and I even learnt later on that they used scissors to cut my face out from all of the family pictures.

So here I was, in a seaside town in England and I happened to be running away from one life, which was the only one I'd ever known, into another life that I was learning about pretty quickly. Thankfully, I got offered a position! Walton Hall was based in Stratford upon Avon, Warwickshire and this was another timeshare resort, which was owned by Graham Maynard who had a secondary resort, El Capistrano Beach Club, which he wanted to complete. He believed that if he sold El Capistrano Beach Club before he had to pay for it, then he would not need to borrow the money from the bank, which would make it cheaper and that's what he did! But the trouble was, when he got enough money to buy the land, the owner decided not to sell it to him! The guy had agreed to sell it to him but then he'd changed his mind, then the next step was to go and acquire another piece of land but he couldn't get one that was available on the beachfront, so he had to go with what was available and he found some land on a hill. Graham had taken all of this money to build a resort and now he had to give it a different name because of its new location but he ensured everyone would get their apartments and what they had paid for. They got what they were promised and also given a special deal but in life, you get some people who like to cause trouble, especially when they do not know the full story. One of these people was Roger Cook, from the British television programme 'The Cook Report'. Roger came round and he became quite aggressive, saying that Graham was a 'con man' and a 'scammer' and he will reveal his lies to the public, which pulled the rug from under Graham's feet! Well, I have worked for him and this was completely untrue, Graham was always determined to give good value for money and what he said he would provide, he honoured his side of the deal.

I continued having wild parties, which was great to drown my sorrows in! And then I had my first ever experience with cocaine. I was at a Soul Festival in Caister, on the north coast of Norfolk, England and I had become friends with one of the organisers, who owned a three bedroom caravan that was on site. This is where I stayed for the bank holiday weekend, Friday through to Monday. Steve and Barry Parker were part of the group that I was with and I was already 'high' with using 'speed' that you bombed and swallowed. It made me feel really happy and at ease and I even remember a moment, where I was playing on a fruit machine and I would just burst out laughing each time that I won! I felt euphoric! Within a few hours, this led onto cocaine because everyone else around, seemed to be using it. So, of course, I joined in! I distinctly remember a naughty moment on this Friday night with a girl, I was clearly filled with drugs by 10pm and she approached me and told me how horny she was feeling! So I took her back to the caravan to enjoy the delights but all of the three bedrooms were occupied by the others having sex. They were all at it! So, we decided to 'do it' on the car bonnet. I will leave the rest to your own imagination. Hedonistic days of complete debauchery and madness, which was helping me to forget all of my problems and what I did not want to face up to.

This is where I met my life long best friend, Stephen 'Stevie G' Grocutt. We worked together, travelling to roadshows and spending many hours drinking in the pubs! During our business trips to London, we would go to Wimbledon Village to enjoy the bars until we were drunk and then drive ourselves home, even after having consumed vast amounts of alcohol! It was just something that most people did back in those days. On one occasion, Stevie parked up his Porsche 911 and we did our usual entertainment. When it was time for us to leave the bar, we stumbled back to where we left the car but it was gone! It had been stolen. Now suddenly alert, Stevie made a call and reported it stolen. His personal belongings were in the car, his house keys, his Filofax and cheque book and credit cards. He managed to get a hire car the next day and our work continued as normal that week, until the following weekend, where we went for another drink in the exact same place. As we were in the bar enjoying our beverages, we both suddenly had a flashback! We did not leave the car where we thought it was, it was somewhere else, so we downed our drinks quickly and decided to go and investigate. We were right! It was there, untouched and waiting for Stevie, to drive it. So, with pride and relief, he turned the key to start the engine but he drove less than a mile before the Police pulled him up and accused him of theft, as the vehicle was registered stolen!

Another time, I was driving on a country lane and I was going around a bend and suddenly there was a tractor in front of me, so I swerved and steered my car into a ditch! The car was on its side and I was a mile and a half away from where I lived. I climbed out of the vehicle and the farmer in the tractor completely ignored me, probably thinking that I was an idiot for driving so fast on a country lane. With the shock I just ran home but as soon as I closed the front door as I was standing there in the hallway, I collapsed! My leg felt really strange and I managed to get to the hospital where they told me, my leg was broken! I had run home on a broken leg! The adrenaline must have driven me home, to where I felt safe and thankfully, I did recover quickly.

This next story was a miracle!

This was another drunken night out and there was a different Steve that was driving us home. When suddenly he lost all control of the car and it went off the road and rolled and rolled and rolled, ten times over. It stopped slap bang in the middle of a field, turned upside down but we managed to clamber out and walk home. We went back the next day, to see what state the car was in and to relay the full impact of our experience. The farmer of the field approached us and shook his head, "They couldn't have survived that accident!" We told him that we were

---

the culprits and shared the whole story from beginning to end. But we never had a bruise or anything damaged, it was truly a miracle! God was certainly looking after me and the lads! I have since then, been amazed at how the physical and mental body can alter in states from being inebriated in one moment and completely sober the next. This occurred to me when one night, when I could barely stand up, I was at the front door of a lodge, that I shared with Simon Roach and it was a gatehouse to a private hall and I was trying to find the opening for the key to go into, when I heard the phone ringing. I somehow managed to open the door and pick up the phone to say hello. It was Lucy letting me know that Lee had been in a car accident and he was in hospital. In a millisecond, the shock of those words sobered me up! I was aware of everything and I was crystal clear again. I drove from Warwickshire to Devon and when I arrived, I was told how Lee was on his skateboard going down a slope and at the bottom of it, there was a road that he had not managed to avoid in time and the car had hit him on the side and Lee went straight through the windscreen! He had hurt his jaw amongst other injuries. An extraordinary thing happened one year later, on the exact date. Glenn, my second son did exactly the same thing! He was on his skateboard and was not able to avoid the road and a car hit him on the side and Glenn also went straight through the windscreen! He was admitted to hospital, with similar injuries to Lee!

Meanwhile back in Torquay, Lucy had made contact with the Child Support Agency (CSA) and eventually, I received a notification from the CSA, to pay Lucy the money for my children. Basically, they chased after me and I was going through the court system. Lucy would constantly say "It's not for me, I need the money for the kids!" And she was 100% right. "They will pay me the money but they will come after you." And with that, they pursued me until I had a final hearing that I had to attend, in Torquay Magistrates Court. I travelled from Stratford on Monday and when I met with my lawyer, he said "You are in trouble here, you have three women magistrates, bend over and kiss your arse goodbye!" With that, they sent me to Exeter prison for six months!

I flew into an internal rage about being sent to prison, as I felt that the situation had now been worsened because I couldn't earn any money, to pay anything back! What benefit is it, to lock the father away from his children? I believe other measures should be offered to the father regarding maintenance issues, the Government system should be giving positive guidance and support to benefit the separated parents and the children.

The trouble is, that when you are in prison, others talk about it as being a University of Crime and that is exactly what it is. I got in with a bad crowd. I appealed and I got out after serving three months of my time, as this was a civil matter and not a criminal matter. When I came out, I tried to get myself back on my feet but started doing things that were classed as 'wrong' financially, I was printing my own credit cards and £20 notes! It was exciting getting away with the things that the lads had taught me in prison, as I would never have known about doing business in this way, if it was not for them! But I was blind to the reality of my actions. The 'game' I was playing did not continue for much longer, I was back in prison for being naughty!

I remember someone named Malky Mullen, he was a Glaswegian car thief and I shared a cell with him. His advice to me was "If you want a peaceful life in prison, remain a number. Don't let them know your name because they are not judgemental, just custodial. There is nothing they can do and if you want to moan, speak to your lawyer or take it to court. That is their contract, only to keep you in custody." It certainly was good advice!

Here I was, 25 years of age with two stints in prison, going through a divorce procedure and being apart from my beautiful children. I can now see that I was far too young to have had so much responsibility. I appealed once again and I was allowed out after a remission. Graham Maynard picked me up from Exeter prison gates in an Aston Martin Vantage Volante and took me back to Stratford upon Avon, where they held a 'welcome home' party for me at the BoatHouse restaurant and bar. The additional celebration was for my magnificent five star sales that actually happened the week before my court case, where I had written one deal each day from Wednesday to Friday and six deals at the weekend! So I had a big pay cheque for my commissions, which I had earned from those months previously! The night got even better! A very eligible woman, whom I shall name 'Bird', I always believed she was way out of my league to ask out for a date but she walked over to me and said "So…you have had three months in prison?" "Yes" I replied. "So that means you have had three months without sex?" she continued. "That's right," I said. "Well, tonight is your lucky night then!" I certainly was a lucky man that night! What a magnificent treat after being locked away behind bars. Bird and I started to see each other more often. She had a huge house and the first time that I went to visit her, her father was waiting for me in the driveway. He proceeded to interview me, about dating his daughter and this was before I could even enter the house! Over the months that we were together, I would visit her home on many occasions and on one particular day, she told me guests were arriving to talk business with her father and I was to sit there and not engage with the discussion. Margaret and Denis Thatcher entered the room. The conversation was about nuclear waste, as Birds' father disposed of this material, for the Prime Minister. It was being sent out to 'third world' countries around Russia that were willing to take it for the right amount of money. To me, it was just getting rid of the problem. Margaret was drinking her cup of tea and I was bored shitless! As I could not participate other than being polite. So, I excused myself and went to the kitchen where Denis followed me and ended up pouring us both a gin and tonic! I can honestly say that he was a nice man, we were getting along and chatting about life and it was certainly more fun than the other conversation! I met Denis and Margaret Thatcher a few more times and I always ended up in the kitchen chatting with Denis, about everything and nothing. In England we use the term about someone being a 'good egg', well, that is how I would describe him.

I was proud to be dating Bird, as she was classed as 'hot property' in Stratford upon Avon. Our relationship lasted only a few months, when one day I said to her "Look, I'm moving to Spain." "When?" she burst out. "Tomorrow" I replied. She went mental at me! We did spend the night together and when I woke up the next morning, Bird had gone and had left me and I spotted a note on the dresser, where my sterling silver Cartier lighter should have been, she wrote "I've taken your lighter, that's the least you owe me, you bastard!" I told her the previous night that I would call her when I got settled in Spain. I completely forgot! It was a decade later when I called her up! We met up and talked about those days but this time, she said to me "If you don't commit to marrying me right now, then I'm not going to sleep with you". I could not bind myself to Bird, so I left and then I met up with her sister for a drink and I had sex with her. I know what you're thinking! I agree, I was a very naughty boy back in those days. Espana, here I come!

24 years old

Stephen 'Stevie G' Grocutt

Aston Martin Vantage Volante

— CHAPTER 5 —
Viva Espana

As the plane landed in Malaga airport, I had a good feeling about my future.

Paul Shanks, was the top manager of Partners in Property from Sunderland, England and alongside him, was Kenny Tokley and they both 'headhunted' Paul Pennicott and myself and offered us both, a good wage to go and work for them, as I was always in the top three in sales, in the UK.

On my first night I travelled to Calahonda which was my new base, in the resort 'La Orquidea' but unfortunately, the staff had left for the evening and the only person that could help me, was a female manager, Terri La Conte. She fully understood my situation and said "You can stay at my house for the night but you have to understand, that I have no interest in having sex with you." My reaction was "Okay, that's fine." I did smile to myself and thought she was kidding! Terri lived with her girlfriend and she offered me the settee to sleep on for the night and then the next day, I got myself ready to return to the resort and have a meeting with Paul who ran the company, which was owned by Russell Foster.

With all of the positive attention surrounding me, I felt like a 'superstar' that had come over from England and as you can guess, my ego kicked in and I continued to party and even forgot, why I ever came over to Spain in the first place. It's true! All I did was party! I had new women each day and alcohol was constantly flowing and cocaine was routine, like a love affair. Some of the lads even had a competition, to see how many days we could go with having different girls each day but after two weeks the challenge became boring, as it was way too easy just to go down to our local bars, see a group of women who were attracted to our money and cars and that was it! My behaviour continued in this manner for six months. There was no love involved, it was just fun to do and my chat up line was 100% guaranteed! I would approach a beautiful female and begin my line, "You'll have to forgive me but you look absolutely stunning…(long pause)…considering" then the next step was to drop my eyes to the floor and walk away from them. Without fail, she would pursue me, tap me on the shoulder and ask "Considering what?" With that cheekiness and my smile, the conversation would flow, as she would either giggle, shake her head at me or roll her eyes! One particular female friend, who was a model said to me "I can't believe that you get away with that! That would not work on me." You guessed it, I set her up! So, I got one of my friends who was a bodybuilder, the type she would generally take a fancy to and I told him to follow my exact procedure. I then went to the toilet and left him to it. My male friend, meandered over to my female friend. He followed the 'plan' of action perfectly, as he tapped her on the shoulder and said to her, "Excuse me love but you look absolutely stunning…(long pause)…considering", dropped his eyes to the floor and walked away. But in that exact moment, I was returning to carry on chatting with him, when my female friend was in pursuit of the body builder and said to him "Considering what?" He responded "Considering you know Charlie!" We all laughed, as she punched my arm and said "You're such a wanker, Charlie!" You see, the trick is to be cheeky, without being offensive, this was the mastery of my technique and it worked for years!

I did meet a well-known 'posh' lady from England, at one of these parties and for fourteen days and nights, we never slept once during that time! The only time we went to bed was for sex, as I fuelled myself with champagne and cocaine and when she returned to England, I was found unconscious in my apartment and taken to the hospital! Obviously my body had taken on too much craziness and I ended up staying there for a week, to reboot my immune system. As the week passed, I was getting fed up and I wanted to return to my lifestyle, as soon as I could. So with that, I checked myself out of the hospital, even dragging the drip with me, which was still attached to my hand! But I did not manage to escape that easily with the medical staff, as they were advising me to stay but I refused to stop any longer, so they had to remove the tube from my hand. I then got a taxi and went home because all I could think of was getting back into the game.

There are some ground rules you have to master before going out to a new bar, to get the best night out. I would decide which venue I wanted to visit and a day or two before, I would go in and introduce myself, to get to know the people who run the place. I would generally ask to meet with the owner, if they were available and find out who was the head of security. My purpose was to inform them of the day that I wanted to come into their venue, with a group of friends and my estimated time of arrival. I would tell them where I would be waiting, for the agreed signal, so we could enter discreetly. I never paid any money on the side, as it was the simplicity of an honest and open conversation and where I would give them good business. I will give you some advice to ensure that you always get great service because this works for me. I always give a 'tip' on my first round of drinks, as this will make sure, you will get served for the rest of the night, as a priority! Don't wait until the end to leave a tip.

With my 'superstar' ego, I was abusing the generosity of the company's expenses, during those first six months and now it had caught up with me and suddenly I was in big trouble at work! I had not done my job or even sold one timeshare, since I had been in Spain and one day, Paul Shanks approached me, grabbed me by the shirt and shoved me up against the wall and said "If you don't do a deal today, I'm gonna knock you out!" From that day, I wrote a deal every single day for thirty consecutive days. I had got my head back in gear, as I pride myself, to be the best at everything I can do and I was not going to let myself down now. I got back into work and did so, for the remainder of my time in Spain.

I was a member of the 'Five Star Club', which was an elite team of salespeople from all over the world and this meant that you had signed five deals, on five consecutive days. Some of us were regulars and we would meet up every month or so, when someone had achieved success for a five star deal. We would get invited to parties all over the place, which were sometimes quite random but I was always willing to pop on a plane, to celebrate any occasion! As you make connections worldwide, you create circles of friendship and acquaintances.

There were about one hundred sales people working together and I shared an apartment, with other lads from the company, Ged McGuirk, Nick Woodham, Norman Anderson and Matthew Evans and we are still good friends. We would work hard all day and party through the night. Our local bars were David's Bar in Riviera del Sol, the London Pub in Fuengirola where we even have our own bottles of Bacardi stacked behind the bar, with our names on because we drank so much of it and it was cheaper to buy it by the bottle! We also enjoyed playing pool, in Calahonda and Fuengirola. Ged, had a girlfriend called Suzy Dodd but because we knew a few Suzy's, we changed it for Soosie. Why? Because she had big boobies and so it was easier to add 'oo' to her name and when we would write her name down, we would add dots in the 'oo' to look like boobs! Silly, but funny and she claimed the title and calls herself that name, to this day.

I had already fallen in love with Spain and I got another brilliant opportunity whilst I was in the resort of La Orquidea and La Cartuja, to become the Project Director, at the Matchroom Country Club. This was perfect for me, as it was linked to snooker and golf, the two sports that I loved. It was also linked to Barry Hearn, of Matchroom in England, he was the founder and chairman, who would come and stay on a regular basis, as this was part of a deal that had been created by Robert & Diane Atkin. I then became good friends with snooker professionals, such as Cliff Thorburn and his wife Barbara, he was known as the 'Grinder' and Willie Thorne and his wife Fiona, Willie was known as 'Mr 147'. We got to know each other so well, that eventually, they left the resort and would stay with me in my villa for privacy. I would also spend a lot of my time with them, on my visits to England. A very special memory was when Barbara, Cliff's wife asked me "What are you doing for your birthday?" I said that I had nothing planned. "You have got to have a party! It's your birthday. Leave it to me, I'll get it done" she said. So, my 31st birthday became my first ever birthday party celebration of my life! Barbara had arranged everything at my house, where they were all staying, what a kind and amazing lady to give me, that special memory.

Sadly, Willie Thorne passed away this year, on June 17th 2020.

Puerto Banus is a Marina and popular with international celebrities and millionaires and as you become more of a local, you get invited to parties and more parties and then other people turn up at your house because they hear that there is a party going on! You tend to attract lots of different characters and it certainly is eye opening! I often left these venues extremely drunk, where I continued to drive my car towards the barrier, coming out of Puerto Banus, where the Police stood by doing their job, of checking on the people, on exit and entry. I was always pulled over but not to give me a threat or a warning, it was just to check if I was okay to drive and if they ever felt that I was not safe to drive home, they would ask me to move over to the passenger seat and take me home! They would stay to party with me because my parties were always the best! Sometimes, they would escort me home and follow me to ensure that I had arrived safely, I was even told "It's amazing, how you can even drive your vehicle!" I replied "I feel more alert, when I'm pissed!"

The Police turn a blind eye to the cocaine, used by known locals but it would depend on your behaviour in public and whether you were out of control, going crazy or showing off about your habits. They wished to manage this, by giving you a little freedom but you do not want to cross or abuse that fine line that they gave you. If you know the fundamental rules, then this makes life smoother and on occasions, I was politely asked to leave venues and go home, which I always respected. The Chief of Police did give me some good advice, "Charlie, do not disrespect the people of Spain. Don't shit on your own doorstep!"

I still get invited to the Police Christmas Ball, as I do give generously because I feel that they are worth their weight in gold, as they have been very supportive to me over the years, that I have lived here. There are some good officers in authority, whom I have great respect for.

With my lifestyle, I never had any savings, as I earnt the money and then spent the money as I went along, it was in one end and out of the other. I found making money really easy and I was happy to change my lifestyle, according to my earnings. If they were higher, I would upgrade my cars and move to a better property, as I found the quality of life, was through renting houses and not buying them, as I did not want to have a mortgage and chain myself to something, that I did not want to be tied down to. I could always downgrade if I was earning less money, it was that simple.

During my time in Spain, I had no communication with my birth family, for a long time. In the beginning, they would still question my choices, intimidate me or try to change my thoughts, into their thoughts. I changed my numbers of contact, to cut my cords with them. I wanted to cleanse myself from the toxic past and start to live the life that I believed in. This certainly took some years to come to terms with and I did eventually speak to them and I still do, but on very rare occasions, as they do not let me forget that they are 'praying for me, to get right again'. I always respectfully say "I have made my choices and I am happy with them, I don't need to come to your church, to believe in God". I did miss them back then but buried my sadness.

My beautiful children Lee, Glenn and Carla came over to spend time with me on a regular basis. Sometimes, they would even travel as unaccompanied minors but most of the time, I would have friends that would bring them on the plane, to see me and even Cliff and Barbara or Willie and Fiona would bring my kids, along with their own children. My relationship with them was still good and improved over the years but they were having a challenging time with Lucy, being a single mum as I was not looking after them, the way a father should have done. I then got a chance of moving back to the UK, so this would mean, me and the kids could spend even more time together each week!

The team decided on doing timeshare roadshows back in England and Paul Shanks, picked the thirty elite sales people, that he wanted to manage the workload and this meant, that we would work on a rota system, of fourteen days on and ten days off but the work was intense, as you could easily manage to perform anywhere up to sixteen hours per day. You certainly needed to reboot yourself, on your days off. We began our roadshows in Bristol and Edgware, North London, which was a satellite office and we also had other offices based in Croydon, Bristol and Manchester.

We did have a scary moment one time! We were on the 13th floor of Imperial House Tower in North London, delivering our sales pitch to a room full of people, when suddenly, three men with masks covering their faces, arrived with a sawn off shotgun! They came into the room calling for the boss. I was the floor manager and they had come to find Paul

Shanks, who had stolen £1,000,000 from Russell Foster and they were coming to collect what they were owed. The room full of clients, ran out of the building in a hurry! The men found Paul in a room and shoved the gun into his mouth, cut his lips and demanded the money back or they would blow his head off! They gave him the opportunity to respond and edged the gun out of his mouth "You haven't got the fuckin bollocks!" He shouted at them. I ran out of that room and down thirteen flights of stairs, faster than you can imagine! I went into a bagel shop, a few doors away, ordered a bagel and just sat there until the dust settled. Later on, Paul told me he wasn't going down, without a fight! But they stole his watch and some money and warned him, they would return a week later but he paid what he owed, before they arrived.

Our team worked hard as they always did, to complete sales and other tasks that were required in the job and after a full day's work, we would head straight down to the pubs and whenever the nightclub was open. In Bristol, on White Ladies Road, we partied there until it closed at 2am. On one particular occasion, after another record breaking day, we were out celebrating, drinking our champagne! I was being quite flashy, when I noticed a group of ladies, eyeing us up! We managed to mingle and one of the women said something to me, so I used one of my cheeky chat up lines, I could not resist the temptation! "You've got something on your chin", as I pointed at my own chin. She touched her chin to see what was there, so she could wipe it away and as she did this, I immediately said "No, the other chin!" "You cheeky fucker! Are you inferring that I am fat?" with a swipe of her hand on my arm. "No, but if you spend the night with me, you will wake up a skeleton!" It certainly worked the charm on Rachel Baker. She was a pretty and curvaceous lady, quite a trophy! As I got to know her, my feelings started to turn into love or at least, what I believed to be love, all those years ago and it was a very different experience for me because Lucy and I were so very young. This time, I was choosing someone, with my own mind and emotions.

During our time together in Bristol, I was approached by Steve and Barry Parker, to see if I wanted to broaden my horizons by selling timeshares in Game Reserves in South Africa, for their company Monteith, Fairchild & Associates, which was based in Rivonia, Johannesburg. This certainly felt like an amazing offer, that I could not turn down!   I told Rachel all about this proposal and that I had already accepted it, she said "Are WE!".   I suddenly thought I wasn't expecting that! "We!" So, I asked Steve and Barry and they said "Bring her, she can be your PA." She was working as an accounts clerk, for an accounting company and she chose to hand in her resignation, so that she could travel over to South Africa with me.

Matchroom Boys

Cliff Thorburn

Soosie Dodd

Willie Thorne

Russel Foster

— CHAPTER 6 —
ADVENTURES *IN* SOUTH AFRICA

We set up our first timeshare, in Sondela Lodge, Warmbaths, situated about one hundred miles north of Johannesburg. This was during 1989, when I happened to have arrived, at this time black people and white people, were officially allowed to share the beaches and swimming pools, publicly. This was deeply etched in history because of the apartheid, which was a system of racial segregation and the country was still adapting to these new experiences, after so much division and separation in the country. Signs similar to, 'Whites Only' were slowly being taken down but they were still dealing with their issues and even in our present times, there are still great changes occurring, for racial harmony to find its balance. Back then, I did go to the swimming pool and was certainly happy to share the pool with anyone but in typical ignorant 'white fashion', no white people showed up. I enjoyed myself though!

Having worked for a time in Sondela, Rachel was my PA but she found it difficult to do as she was told, so I ended up firing her after only one week! She stayed in South Africa as my girlfriend but not as my PA.

I started to understand 'The Bush' mentality and the tribalism between the tribes of the Zulu, Xhosa, Venda people, Tswana and many others. There is a saying, 'That you can take the black man out of the bush but you will never take the bush, out of the black man.' This reigns true, for any culture as its core essence and when you are active, within that culture, this is where you experience it fully and see life, from an alternative perspective and I loved these people. It was so simple, that these ethnic groups didn't want white or any other people going into their communities and ordering them to live life, by their demands. Sadly, this is ancestral and has been in their lineage, for them to be overruled. I can give an example, such as when authority will enter their land, village or town, without any permission beforehand, build a school to force them, to educate themselves under their teachings and jurisdiction and if they disagree, they will demolish the building, as they did not request it in the first place, those people would be considered barbarians or wild people for not accepting, the governments' apparent generosity. The tribes wish to choose their own lifestyles and be independent, from the 'white men' and their tyranny. They wish for freedom, to be who they truly are.

Absolutely, nothing wrong with that!

Soweto, was an area that I was advised not to go into, because it was far too dangerous for me but I went in, with a pure soul and an open heart and I also ensured that I was with the right people, so there was no risk to me at all. If you go to these people, with the intention of changing their beliefs and way of living, then there is a good chance that you may not come out alive. They stick together, and rightly so.

The River Club was an absolutely beautiful place to live in. I was close to The Wanderers Golf Club, which has a well-known golf course, cricket club, snooker club and a fantastic sports facility. As I loved golf, I played there regularly each week. There was a specific area, that looked similar to a cage where the caddies would be waiting for duty and on my first visit to the club, I was given Winston, as my personal caddie and he walked around the golf course in his bare feet, pulling my clubs along with him and doing everything a caddie is meant to do and he appeared to be a nice man. Generally, after 9 holes, you would take a break because of the intense heat and have some refreshments and food. I looked at Winston and said "What do you fancy to eat?" He ordered steak, eggs, chips, it was a plate full! Whilst we sat there eating our food, in the dining area, I noticed people watching me, out of the corner of their eye or giving me strange looks. I was told afterwards that I was only meant to feed my caddie, with a piece of bread and a boiled egg! But, I was glad with my choice because I was doing what felt right for me to do and from then on, Winston became my regular caddie and we continued to eat in the café. I did notice something else, when I played golf with Winston by my side, that when I hit my ball into the rough, by the time I had reached it, it was sitting in a perfect spot. Exactly where I would have wanted it to be and not where I believed it had landed. It was suddenly, no longer behind a tree or no longer buried, the ball was just sitting there waiting for me, in its perfect position. It's amazing what a good meal does for a caddie! "Was it fair play with Winston?" Probably not but over the years, I have often thought of Winston and how amazing he was. My handicap was down, officially back in those days, at 2.8 handicap playing 3, which is a fairly good standard. If you saw me standing on the golf course, you would have seen me dressed, in all of the best golfing attire you could buy and Winston would be there with, no shoes and simple clothing. Then one day he asked me "Can I hit your driver?" "Of course you can!" I said and handed him my driver. He takes hold of the driver, with no glove and he hits it straight down the middle of the fairway! Which was probably, even fifty metres more than I could have hit it, he effortlessly smashed it! We looked at each other and he must have seen the amazed expression on my face and he simply smiled at me. He had a zero handicap, which makes him an amazing player. He was a wonderful human being and was great company. On another day, as we chatted, I told him how I loved playing snooker and he told me, that he could get me on the local team. It was arranged and I went along to the snooker room, in the Wanderers Club and as I played, they realised that I played to a good standard. I had the chance to set the balls up on the table for a game but as I was doing this, a man came up to me at the table, moved me aside and just took over and changed the 'set up', right in front of me. The Green, Brown and Yellow balls, have a specific setting on the snooker table, (mnemonic memory as G"od – B"less – Y"ou) but he rearranged the balls to Yellow, Green and Brown and told me '2,3,4'. We disagreed but there was no convincing him that he was wrong. Over time, I got the chance to play in a competition and as we were waiting for the referee, to set up the balls on the table, I looked over at the man who thinks they should be set up as '2,3,4', I caught him rolling his eyes and shaking his head at the referee for arranging the balls, in what he believed to be the wrong position. Obviously, the whole world had got it wrong. I did chuckle to myself!

Mabula Lodge was a stunning game reserve that I got involved with and I loved to work from my tree house, which was built on stilts. It really was wonderful and so peaceful, to sit there and do my work with the windows open, as I listened to the sounds of nature and sometimes even a cheeky monkey or two would come in, to investigate what this place was. On one particular day, a giraffe decided to poke his head through one of the openings! I never realised how big their heads were, until that precise moment. I nearly jumped out of my skin!

In the evenings, we would go to the watering hole, to see all of the animals gathering in large numbers together, to lap up the water. It was such a magical setting, with nature, the elements and observing the pecking orders, of the various animals and how they reacted to each other, was utterly fascinating to see and as the sun was setting, it was a completely heart expanding experience.

So many stunning places come to mind like, Mabalingwe, Sanbonanni and Sabi Sabi, were equally outstanding in beauty and magnificence. The Northern Transvaal, was deeply historical, as too, the south coast of Africa and Cape Town with its heritage and sculptures. My eyes opened to the diverse wildlife and native animals, such as the Kudu, which is a type of antelope.

I loved the Braais (barbeques), which you cannot compare to a British barbeque! We ate various types of meats, such as ostrich and they are marinated with savoury sauces and assorted delicacies, such as biltong that is meat, cured and dried. My favourite sauce, that had the most unusual name, was 'monkey gland' sauce! What are your immediate thoughts? Well, I thought the same thing! But it's not made, from any monkeys or from any glands, it's just a marketing name.

During my visit to one of the game reserves, a guy from Durban turned up on a game reserve, in his private helicopter and with his film crew. Apparently, their intention was to film Rambo, who was a local 'famous' elephant! They landed their helicopter as close as they could get to him, so they could video some action shots. But, the locals knew that Rambo was unpredictable and he performed perfectly, when he continued to move towards the helicopter, he backed into it and crushed it! Maybe he had some vengeance? But you can imagine how suddenly vulnerable all of those men must have been feeling, with nowhere to run to and a helicopter that was now unavailable for them, to make a quick departure. Suffice to say that within 24 hours the word had spread far and wide and all of the local people got to hear of the news, of the one and only legend, Rambo.

Swaziland, is a country within a country and the capital city is Mbabane, I visited The Hilton Garden Inn Hotel, for an overnight stay and as I spoke to the receptionist, she informed me that the hotel was full, she appeared to be local and I asked to speak to the manager, as I know that hotels can keep some rooms aside for moments like these. His name was Angus Fraser, a Scotsman and this lovely man offered me the wedding suite, for the night!

Sun City is a luxurious resort with casinos and is in a separate territory, called Bophutatswana which was reincorporated back into S. Africa, in 1994. It is owned and was developed by my good friend of mine, Sol Kerzner and I remember his right hand man Barboza, who was quite flashy and you could not miss the various watches that he wore on one arm, which showed other time zones! He even designed his watch face, with his own face made specifically for him by Rolex!

Johannesburg is the largest city in South Africa and one fascinating fact, is that it's roughly 5,900 feet above sea level, which means the air is thinner and because of the reduced oxygen, the car engines are made bigger, e.g.: in Britain, a Ford Fiesta Escort and Sierra would be in the style of an XR2, XR3 and XR4 but in Johannesburg you would have the XR4, XR6 and XR8. Obviously, that's if you have any interest in cars and their designs!

I can share a final story with you but I choose not to reveal any of their names, as I have respect for their families. Two other people travelled alongside me on this trip and they were given guns, to shoot any 'niggers' freely! They both found humour in this concept and they did use their weapons on some human beings. I was also given a gun, with ammunition to do the same thing but I locked it away in the safe, as I was disgusted by this and as Karma always has the final say, they were both hit by ricochet bullets from the weapons that were used, in a robbery by a gang, in a bank in Johannesburg and they were both killed! It is a heart-breaking story, in different ways but it's the truth, that is raw and real and the sadness is, that this still can happen in our modern times.

I had been here for nearly 8 months and achieved great success, with the timeshare resorts. It was a privilege to have been invited to this country and it holds a special place in my heart, thank you South Africa, my time was coming to an end, to return back to England.

Rachel and I had been dating for about twelve months and I decided to ask her to marry me! Rachel said to me that she could not marry me, unless I moved permanently back to England because she knew what to expect, with my busy life, as I travelled backwards and forwards around England, Spain and S. Africa. This was a big commitment for me to take on and it would mean a complete change of lifestyle but I believed that I would be happily married, so I agreed to her request and I chose to give up the timeshare business and look forward to starting afresh. As Rachel had resigned from her job, she was not sure what to do when she got back to England but she did tell me that her dream would be to train, as an air hostess for Virgin Atlantic Airlines, so I told her to follow her dream and she did.

Our Wedding reception was at the Royal Crescent Hotel in Bath and we were joined, by Rachel's adoptive parents Howard and Maureen Baker, from Mangotsfield, to celebrate our marriage ceremony. They are absolutely wonderful people, I would call them the 'salt of the earth' and I had the pleasure of them being my new family. Every Sunday, Howard went to church, even though he did not believe in God! And when I asked him why he went to church, even though he did not believe in God, he told me, he only went as an 'insurance policy', just in case there was one!

Whites only

Rambo

Monkey Gland Sauce

— CHAPTER 7 —
Back to Bristol

I was 30 years old and unemployed and I knew that it was going to be a challenge for me to find work, that would be fun, enjoyable and for it to pay me good money. I was now job hunting as a married man, who had decided to settle down in Bristol.

A closed-circuit television company, called Camera, had a vacancy available and I managed to get an interview with them, at their Yate office near Bristol. I was interviewed by the sales manager Mr David Brown. Camera, was bought out by a larger company called Sensormatic, whose head office was in Harefield House, Hertfordshire and the company sold closed circuit electronic surveillance systems, for businesses. During my interview, I noticed that they were not really keen to give me the position, as I had no previous expertise in this type of sales and the background was very different, to what I was used to selling. But thankfully, the manager at that time, David Brown, saw something in me that he liked and he believed, there was a good chance it could work in their favour and with that, I got the position!

The company required me to reach my annual sales targets, of £147,000 gross margin, which is the profit for the company and in my first week of working for them, they gave me the worst street in Bristol to be a sales rep, it was on Gloucester Road! I had to knock on doors and sell these surveillance cameras but it was a street that all sales reps hated! It was a great challenge to sell anything in this area because it was full of corner shops and Asian people. There is nothing wrong or bad with the people, community or businesses. It was because they are united and only deal with who they know and trust, as they are a close knit community, which I truly admire and they look after themselves and each other, which is wonderful but not for a complete stranger, called Charlie, who is trying to sell them a brand new product! But, I did spot a door that I knew, no one had knocked on before. It was HM Bristol Prison and they let me in! I asked to speak to the Governor and they agreed. I got the opportunity to show Bob Dixon, my cameras and monitors and he said "Boy, the quality of that is so much better than the shit, we've got in here!" I agreed, it was old fashioned, it was ancient, it had black and white images and I was selling HD quality in colour. He really wanted to see how he could strike a deal with me, as his first thoughts, where to put the cameras in the visitor's area but he did have a budget to follow. I continued to show him everything, in detail and how it all worked and he loved it, as the current cameras he had, in the visitor section, showed very little and the images were not clear.

Now, the average order size, back in those days, would estimate at £4-5,000 for each individual order that was placed, which would include the cameras, monitors, surveillance, maintenance, contracts, etc. I walked out of the prison, with an order for £45,000! I was quite chuffed with myself, as you can imagine. Once the system was installed, Bob fell in love with it so much and on my next visit I asked him "What else do you need me to do for you, Bob?" We then put together a plan for the whole of the prison, the kitchens, wings, perimeters, exercise yard, etc. Section by section, without exceeding his budget. Over time, this was complete, with the cameras being fully installed, throughout the whole prison. Our friendship grew over this period of time and I asked him, which other prison would need my services and equipment. He suggested HM Exeter Prison. "No, not that one! That's where they locked me up, when I was younger!" I remarked.

So, as nervous as I was, of being recognised by anyone, I met up with the Governor, Toby Neuth. I walked into his office and headed towards him bravely and when he looked up at me, he said "I know you." 'Oh, shit!' I thought in a moment of panic.

Me: "Yes I was in this prison."

Toby: "I remember you, you should never have been here."

Me: "I thought that I was the only one, who was thinking the same thing."

Toby: "For a non-payment of maintenance money, as a civil matter, I've never heard of that before."

Me: "I must have been the first one then."

Toby: "Then you came back, about 9 months later, as I remember correctly."

Me: "Yeh, I got in with a bad crowd whilst I was inside and the lads taught me how to print credit cards and £20 notes. It seemed like fun at the time, to be making your own money! But, I have learnt the error of my ways now and I have also learnt where your weak spots are, Toby."

Toby: "I'm intrigued, do tell me."

Me: "Well, with the cameras that you've got installed, you are not covering that… that… or that... You need to be doing this…this… and this..."

Toby: "I like that idea!"

So, we started off, doing exactly the same method that I had done with HM Bristol Prison. Stage by stage and all in accordance with his budget. Toby was a character, imagine he's wearing a monocle, with a deerstalker's hat and a little older fashioned in his ways. On one visit, I spotted a cannabis plant on his windowsill.

Me: "What are you doing with that?"

Toby: "One of the inmates gave it to me."

Me: "Do you know what type it is?"

Toby: "I like the flowers, it's a nice plant."

Me: "It's a cannabis plant!"

Toby: "What do you mean?!"

Me: "You didn't know what kind of plant it was?"

Toby: "No! I had no idea."

I laughed so much and he joined in, as he did find the humour in this, as it was obviously given to him as a joke.

When all the cameras had been fully installed, throughout the prison, I asked the same question "Which prison do you recommend, for me to approach next?" He suggested HM Prison Dartmoor.

Today, you would call this 'networking' but it can also be an additional boost with sponsorships, which is supported with funding, for the encouragement to increase business, so for example, Bob, wanted a play area for the children to be in, whilst the parent visited their partner. So, to support him, we have to help each other out, it works both ways in business. You will always get negative people, who say this is bribery or blackmail but I will compare it to fishing, as an analogy. 'If you have nothing on your hook, you catch nothing. If you get the best quality of bait, that you can buy and put it on the end of your hook, knowing exactly what you want to catch, before the line goes in the water, then this gives you a better chance of getting what you want to catch.' Our modern times are very different in these methods, as the banks and bigger businesses limit and restrict any ideals you may have, as they are so rigged against any success or sustainable longevity. So, I would 'network' by inviting the Governors to meet somewhere like, a golf course or something similar. You get to understand each other and the business that they are in and you get to learn more about them, like their frustrations, limitations, requirements, ideals, etc. and this gives you both, open options of service. It's not going through the back door, as this will only depend on your initial intention and who you are as an individual. It's always great going out with different types of people and just spending time away from work and generally socialising, which appears to be abhorrent in the present society, as there is too much opposition and fear with, 'can I trust them' scenarios.

At Sensormatic Camera, I worked with Steve Hughes, my friend and colleague and he was desperate to get into the Government Communications Headquarters (GCHQ) in Cheltenham, which is an intelligence and security organisation, responsible for providing signals intelligence and information assurance to the government and armed forces, of the United Kingdom. He could never get in there, to see the person in authority or someone at the 'top of the tree'. And one time, he said to me "I don't know how you manage to get in all of these prisons." I told him that there's 'ways' to get your foot in the door. So, we agreed to a method that he could try, to reach his goals but he kept failing. I offered my assistance, even going as far as arriving as him! "Look, if you've struggled that much, I will do it for you because I can get in there, you know I always do!" I shared with him one key element: "You must arrive in the office early, like 7.30-8am, you then have a better chance of getting to the top guys, before the secretary arrives because she is paid to keep people like you, away from them!" Alas, the plan did not work out for him. So, the next step was for me to join him and use my magical skills. We agreed on a date to go to the office together and the day arrived, it was 8am in the morning and we now had attracted a large audience of staff members, from the office, as they wanted to see if I was full of shit! They were hoping I would fail, for some morning entertainment. I was certainly put on my toes, with them all watching me perform, so I picked up the phone and dialled the number, the secretary answered. Confidently, I asked her "Is James there please?" She asked who I was and I responded "It's Charlie." She then put me straight through, to James! I couldn't believe it!

James: "Hello Charlie. How are you doing?"

Me: "I'm fine thanks, I've been asked to call you by the Home Office, to discuss security cameras and access control systems. I'd like to pop over and discuss it with you, whenever it's convenient."

James: "Which Charlie's this? Who are you? You're not supposed to be put through to me"

Me: "I'm Charlie Ward"

James: "Oh, I'm sorry, I thought you were my brother!"

As fate would have it, his brother was called Charlie! When the going gets tough, the tough get lucky! He said "As you have managed to get through to me, I cannot do anything but see you now. I want to see the person that has managed to get past my secretary, I wish to meet with you Charlie." The door had been opened for me to step through. I finalised the conversation "Can you ensure that your decision makers, finance directors and technical experts are available for me, on the day of our meeting please? I know how busy you must be and we can do this all in one day and I'll bring my team along, to discuss everything that is necessary."

With an agreed date, Steve and I gathered a team from Warrington and on that day, we delivered a presentation with all we needed and everything at hand. Even when we were challenged or picked out on certain details, we had every positive response for them. It was not my contract, it was Steve's contract and I just opened the door for him, with the original phone call, which led to this moment in time and it was a great success. When the meeting was nearly over, James pulled me to one side and asked for my support with something. I agreed to help him and I was taken to Lansdowne in Bath where I had travelled, with a man from GCHQ. We arrived in a car park and I noticed roughly, up to two hundred vehicles parked up and I saw a square building in the centre, of the private car park and I wondered if it was some type of 'park and ride'. So, we parked the car, I got out and walked towards the building and when the door opened, the first thing that I spotted was a man, sat behind a reinforced glass plate, similar to what you might see in a bank, for complete security and to the right side of me, there was a door. I followed the instructions and handed in my identification card and my Military of Defence pass and it was taken from me, checked and validated and then, they opened the door to my side. I moved forward and saw that it was a lift and the space inside was an estimated twelve square feet, in dimension. It was big and dark and felt cold and a little eerie. The lift was key operated by the guard but it was impossible to know how far you were actually going down but I can only guess, up to two hundred metres below ground and when it reached a 'floor', the guard changed the key and we went down even further! Finally when we arrived, at what I believe to be the bottom floor, the doors opened and I literally was stunned for a moment, by what I was seeing. I was looking at a vast tunnel with massive walls that were white in colour, the ceiling was huge and curved in structure. People were driving vehicles around, that reminded me of golf buggies and they had roads which were wide and had different lanes and there were lots of tunnels, going to different destinations. Well, my eyes were seeing £££ and lots of it! We could put cameras everywhere down here, I was thinking to myself.

But, they only wanted cameras for the access and exit points. I spotted some enormous vaults and asked about them, the guide took us inside one of them and told me that they were used for signalling and messaging during WWII and storing ammunition. They also said that thousands of people would have worked down there with shops, bars and restaurants, a bit like an underground city and this apparently was before GCHQ. To me, it was like a parallel universe, it's like seeing something from a movie, come alive right before your eyes and I had just seen something, that I never knew actually existed! When it was time for us to leave, I just got back into the car and we left this strange place behind. I got on with life and forgot all about it, until I was asked again, to go to another similar place, which was also near Bath.

Recently, some people I know pointed out these places and they said that all they could see, was a housing development being built upon that area and it was owned by the Military of Defence.

I continued my work of sales, in the prisons and during my first month I had managed to beat my annual target and reached £300,000! Because of this phenomenal success, I was suddenly asked to go and meet the directors and chairman of the company. I arrived and was led into the boardroom, where fifteen Directors were seated, Dawson Buck was at the head of the table and the other board members were sat either side of him, seven to the left and seven to the right. I had no prior warning as to why I was called to the Head Office and it seemed like my training officer had obviously thrown me in at the deep end! They all turned to look in my direction and Dawson, the C.E.O spoke to me "Charlie Ward, you have done an amazing job and your numbers are off the scale! Could you tell me, the key to what your success is?" I was extremely nervous and completely unprepared and I looked straight at him and said "If I told you that, then you'd be as good as me!" And with that, I walked out of the room and within half an hour, I was in the car park by my car, when suddenly a hand landed on my shoulder! It was Dawson. He said to me "You and I are going to be friends for a long time, I like you." We have now been friends for thirty years and he has been a rock for me during all of this time. He is one of the most important people that I have in my life and now he is my Godfather and I am Godfather to two of his children. Charlotte called Charlie and Oliver called Ollie, two extremely special people in my life.

Over those years, I visited all of the prisons in the United Kingdom. I was the individual for designing the system, at HM Prison Whitemoor, Cambridgeshire and this was rated as a, Category 'A' prison, which means high security. In the United Kingdom prisoners are divided into four types of security and the higher the category, the worse the convictions are. In Whitemoor, they had a prison within a prison specifically, for extremely high risk prisoners. The day we finished and completed installing the camera system, one of the prisoners escaped! The tale involved twin brothers and a change of identity and it must have been embarrassing, as it did not reach the mainstream media and all I can say is, that their story is just that, a story. This just shows you, that it does not matter how brilliant the system is, if the people operating it do not follow the instruction manual!

When I visited HM Prison Cookham Wood, Kent, Myra Hindley made me a cup of tea!

HM Bristol Prison

Sensormatic Camera

Underground bunker

Ollie and Charlie, my Godchildren

Dawson Buck, my Godfather

— CHAPTER 8 —
LIFE *IN* PRISON

Prison visits were fascinating and I had many experiences but some were more memorable, than others.

I had a meeting, with the Governor of HM Prison Cookham Wood, to offer my camera services and during my time there, a lady served me tea and biscuits, as I chatted away with the female Governor. The woman serving my tea was an older lady, who only spoke to me, to ask if I wanted sugar or milk in my tea or any biscuits to eat. I remember that she was a medium build but frail and her looks were average, she was calm and quiet in her manner. It was only afterwards when I got in my car that I realised who she was, it was Myra Hindley, who was infamous for the Moors murders in the 1960's and she was in prison for life. She was obviously the Governor's gofer and it's always interesting to see these people in person, as you put a face to a name. I was never there in judgement, just to complete my job and detach from the surroundings.

When you go to prison for life, apparently you realise soon enough, that this is going to be long term and at some point, you become calmer and settle down and accept your new way of life and just get on with your existence, and 'Do your bird' as they say. That is how you tell the difference with inmates because when their sentences are shorter or if they are gangs, things kick off and trouble is all around, it's only the lifers, who are quieter.

Another high security unit for males only, is HM Prison Woodhill.

I can only share with you what my experience was in any situation and in this prison, I remember a powerful man, walking around an association area and as it's a high risk prison, the numbers are smaller in groups. I saw about four men, in this area and this one particular man, certainly carried a presence and an air of authority but he looked in good shape, as he was walking around, like he owned the place, which did feel quite intimidating. I also observed his internal anger, like an energy. He was the famous Charles Bronson, an English criminal, who has been referred to by the British press, as the "Most violent prisoner in Britain" and as "Britain's most notorious prisoner".

HM Prison Dartmoor, is positioned right in the middle of Dartmoor and as it's out in the open elements, it was bloody cold! It did have a sense of strangeness, being so out in the open but it was a very interesting place to work.

HM Prison Swansea, on Oystermouth Road, is in the middle of Swansea and on the seafront! It had the lowest wall of any prison in the UK and I was invited to a night of 'video horse racing', where we would socialise, have drinks and gamble. You would enter through, the two main doors and then further along, there were two more doors inside, like a tunnel. They were wide open when you arrived, to drive straight through and once all of the cars were in, they shut the doors, so you were safe, as all of the prisoners had already been locked up early, for the night. It was an entertaining evening with the governors, we had fun.

I got to know the Governor, from HM Prison Gloucester, during my visits. He also had a gofer (Red Band) that I had met whilst visiting the Prison. The Governor would commend him and say what a wonderful role model he was and that he was a beautiful young man and in my thoughts, I am questioning how can a 'lifer' be nice?! But I got to learn some of the lads' story. It was an incredibly sad situation and you can make up your own judgments, as to whether he should be in prison or not. He had been sexually abused by his father, since he was a baby and it was all he ever knew. His mother was a prostitute and she would put him outside of the house, no matter his age or what the weather was, whilst she entertained her clients.

As you can imagine, he was not treated with care, affection, attention or love and this is all a child wants from its parents. He was treated very badly and over time, his internal rage was building up, until it finally exploded, enough was enough and he shot and murdered his mother and his father. This was why he was in prison for life and this, was all of the information I learned about him and I am sure, there was much more than that, which I didn't know about, with his other experiences in life, whether it was from his parents or other people. I actually tried to 'save' him because I could empathise with him, understanding his decision, to kill his parents like that, so that he could end his suffering and everything, they were doing to him. I wanted to help him to get released from prison but I was asked not to go ahead with these thoughts. This young man said to me "Please don't take me out of here, for the first time in my life, I feel safe." He had obviously never known what security was until he arrived in prison. A heart-breaking story but now he is 'happy' with his incarceration.

It's amazing how being behind prison bars can become one's freedom.

Myra Hindley

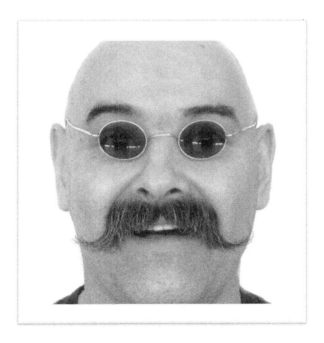

Charles Bronson

CHAPTER 9

CELEBRATING BRISTOL LIFE

Signs are all around us and not just the ones you can see that give you directions to places but those kinds of signs that are more like an internal knowing or gut feeling. It's just whether you choose to listen to them or not!

As a birthday gift for Rachel, I wanted to give her an extra special treat, so I bought her a Honda Civic sports car, in the colour blue. Unfortunately, she did not like the colour I had got and she wanted the colour red, as she was working for Virgin Atlantic and wanted the exact same colour, as the Virgin logo. So, I did what she wanted and I changed it for a red one but there were some alarm bells going off inside of me but I could not really hear them clearly and I dismissed it as nonsense and forgot all about it. I just thought that I knew all about her favourite things but it appeared, that I didn't know her as well as I thought I did.

This did ring true, further down the line, when I was told by some of our close friends, that they believed she was having an affair, with one of the Pilots that she worked with and naturally, I confronted her about what I had heard but Rachel denied this accusation, claiming that her and the man in question, were nothing more than friends but something inside of me, was telling me it was true and part of me, did not want to end our relationship because I wanted safety and security with someone, as I had failed previously with Lucy and had let her down and our three children, so I was holding onto something that turned out not be true anymore. Our marriage finally broke down as it was true, Rachel was having an affair that she had previously denied. I only found out after the breakup, that none of my children actually liked her. Carla told me that she did not like Rachel because she would not give her any pudding, until she had finished her peas! Our marriage lasted for five years and we had no children together, as we both worked full time and had no desire to add, to what we already had together. We did own a house and had lots of friends as a couple and I may surprise you, to tell you, that I found this part quite difficult and with all of these deep emotions whirling through me and also having the circle of people around me, dissolve overnight.

When the relationship had ended, she moved out of the house and we were in the proceedings, of dividing its contents and the sale of the property, in our divorce. But, after I returned home from a trip down to the London office, all I could see in front of my eyes, was that everything was black and empty, nothing was left there anymore and the house was completely burnt out, with my entire life's possessions. A neighbour approached me "Do you know you had a house fire?" "Well, I can see that now." I said clearly. The insurance company was really good with me. They put me up in a hotel, for a few nights and told me to buy some clothes, as all I had was what I was standing up in. When you have a house fire, that destroys your whole entire contents, these simple things you can take for granted and then you suddenly realise, that you don't have it anymore. It truly hit me like a train.

Apparently, there had been an electrical fault in the kitchen that had ignited itself to create the cause of the fire. Rachel felt that I had done this on purpose, to get rid of my memories of her and our relationship. The fire was very symbolic for me, as this part of my life was now gone, burnt out and it was time to start afresh, once more.

I found an apartment to rent, in Clifton Village, Bristol. I had luxurious white carpets and I made sure I only drank champagne, so it would not mark the carpets! It was time to find some new friends and go out alone, which I did and eventually, I bumped into some guys, who were all very close friends and suddenly it was this complete stranger that they had taken under their wings, as true gentlemen. It was so lovely to know that they had all grown up together and they are still, my good friends, Geoff Bracey, Paul Ambrose, Mark Johnson Allen, Ian Hutchinson, Richard Boot and Wayne Tatlock. In those days, we had joined David Lloyds Tennis Club, to play sports and occupy myself, as I socialised and met other people that were just as competitive as me, at playing tennis. I met Guy Kelland, who was quite similar to me, as a cheeky chap and one time after our game had finished, I asked him if he wanted a second beer.

Guy: "No thanks, I have to be up early in the morning."

Me: "So do I."

Guy: "Yeah but I have to drive down to Torquay."

Me: "So have I."

Guy: "Why? Have you got a boat down there?"

Me: "Yes I have."

Guy: "So do I!"

When we got to Torquay, it turned out that our boats were side by side!

On the weekends, I would go out on my boat and take my children with me, we would all have such great fun, water skiing and doing many more activities together. My boat was an American Cruiser Rogue named 'R U Firkenshore'! And being the comedian that I can be, I met another comedian, who had a boat called Champagne Charlie! It was Jim Davidson, an English stand-up comedian.

Guy had a professional water-skiing boat and when we went out together on our boats, it was like a smooth marriage, as we would put all of the people on my boat and water-ski off his boat, we became great friends. He had a girlfriend called Heather and as a couple, I could only describe them as a schoolboy and schoolteacher. Some of the lads, even had a bet on, them only lasting for a couple of months but they are still together, after all of these years, as man and wife and they are beautiful people. We were having so much fun one summer that we would finish work in Bristol and head off to Torquay from Friday until Sunday. But as it's in our nature to be naughty boys, this led us to having longer weekends, which meant us going down on a Thursday until Sunday. This extended to Thursday to Monday and by the end of the summer, we ended up only going into work on a Wednesday!

I want to share one of those truly memorable moments. Glenn, my second son was about 16 years of age and he was my only child, who had not yet learned how to water ski. Paul Ambrose who is a dear friend and a brilliant water skier, had already taught Lee and Carla, not just how to ski but to ski very well. On this particular occasion, we were having lunch in a bay, in Torquay and we had finished eating our food and we were getting ready to leave, when Glenn suddenly spots a girl from school that he really fancies and suddenly turns to Paul and says urgently "I want to ski right now! Right now from this spot outwards!" "But you haven't done it before!" Paul exclaimed. "I can do it!" he burst out with complete confidence. We jumped on the boat and please do remember, that this is the first time Glenn has even put himself in this position on the water, he had only ever watched us ski. This girl that he has eyes for, is watching every move of Glenn and the only thing he can do now, is to impress her. He came straight out on the water, just like he had done it a million times before! Wow! The smile on his face was as wide as a Cheshire cat. My mouth was wide open and I was stunned watching him out there on the water. My boy had done it! He was a complete success! But now, he was locked in this position and he could not let go of the handles because his arms had frozen to them! He carried on skiing for another thirty minutes, until he had the courage to let go. I was truly proud of Glenn. I don't think the girl he fancied waited around for him though. Some you lose!

Paul Ambrose surprised me one time! I was out with Guy, visiting some of his family in Torquay and the house was situated in a lovely position, where I was admiring the beautiful view with a drink in my hand, when suddenly to my horror, I saw my boat in the water going out of the harbour! Paul was at the wheel! Well, I did have a moment of panic watching my own boat leave the harbour with me, not at the boat's wheel!

I had always had a supply of champagne, on the boat and various types of alcohol. I did notice on some occasions, that one or two bottles would disappear and I would spot an empty condom packet, lying around on the floor. I would ask my boys about what I had found and that champagne had been used but they would deny everything. But I definitely knew it was not Carla. I did have quiet moments of pride as a dad because they were wise to use a condom and enjoy quality booze, so I know that Lee and Glenn did entertain women on the boat, a bit like a father, like son! I did have a feeling that their mother would disapprove of their behaviour and we never mentioned it to her.

As I had my new boat, I made up a new chat up line, so when we were out clubbing in Torquay, I would sidle up to a beautiful woman and say "Do you want to come and sit on my boat?!" We were a bit crazy and many times, we water-skied naked because we had no swimwear, as we had gone straight to the boat from the nightclub and we were usually pissed and naturally, not behaving normally. I was starting to live life to the full again!

I dated Jane Ray for a few months but then I felt it was time to end our relationship. Shortly after this, I was in 'Wedgies' nightclub on Park Street, Bristol when Suzy Ray, Jane's sister jumped in front of me and verbally attacked me, she may have even given me a slap on the arm because she was really upset with me, for finishing with her sister. In a bizarre way, after some weeks of seeing each other at the same venues, we actually became good friends, Suzy and I. It was approaching her 30th birthday and she was feeling very sad because her boyfriend had recently dumped her and she asked me if I could hold a party for her, at my place, to cheer her up. "Of course I will" And I did just that. It was a great evening and at midnight we had a present giving moment, where I had bought her two gifts. One was a 'shelf', representing being single and left on the shelf! And the second gift was extra special and I told her, she was only allowed to use it from Monday to Friday. I had bought her five different types of vibrators, one for each day of the week, as I knew she would not need them at the weekend!

We became great buddies and she even rented a room from me, for a few months. One night, she decided to go out on a date and she left all glamorous and excited to meet this guy. When she came home, she had brought her date back with her and I was waiting for her reaction and it did not take long, before I heard her scream "Charleeeee!!!" I had very carefully put a porno magazine under her duvet cover, which sat neatly next to a 12" black vibrator! I laughed and went back to bed. She still has not told me what happened next! But I do know that she loves me.

I was ready for a short break away and I felt a holiday was due and thankfully my good friend Sally Evans, was available to join me in Tenerife. Whilst we were there, we met a lovely couple, Lee and Jeanine Clarson and it was fascinating to learn about their dance wear clothing company, which provided unique and glamorous designs for television shows. They were on holiday with their daughter Mia, aged 4 and she and I became friends, as we went on a few outings together to give her parents a break as she talked nonstop! Asking questions and questions, "Why do you do this?" "What's that?" She was curious about everything and needed explanations about the world! She was such a delight to be with.

Water skiing was always brilliant fun when I went out with the lads and Dominic Baldwin, was someone I met through Guy and Heather and I remember how he was always very careful with his money. He had purchased a boat and made the decision, not to use petrol but gas. It was a MasterCraft, where he could use the gas conversion into LPG, which meant that it would save you money in the long run. Sadly though, when we were out on Lake Windermere, he was getting short on gas and there was no access to this facility but there were plenty of petrol stations locally! Suffice to say, he was not impressed.

This was hilarious! Not about Dominic but my next tale.

Me and some lads had met up to take another trip out on the water together. Before we set off, we were joking around, talking about how cold it was up at Lake Windermere because of its depth. It's well known for this and we joked, about how we could warm ourselves up by doing a little wee in our wetsuits, to get some temporary heat. One of the men had no attire for skiing, so we said to him, "That's no problem, we'll sort something out for you to use." There was no spare wetsuit but we found a dry suit for him to use. Now, the differences are, that a wetsuit is like a second waterproof skin, where you can squeeze it over your bathing suit, underwear or go naked if you prefer! A dry suit goes over your full clothing and seals around the wrists, ankles and neck. With all of our gear organised, we headed off for some fun and forgot about this conversation. So, when this guy gets into the water, we hear him call out "I can't feel myself getting warm?" We shout back to him "What do you mean?" He said "I've had a pee in my suit because you told me I would get warm!" We were in hysterics. "We told you it only works with a wet suit. You've got a dry suit on, which means you've gone and pissed yourself!"

I met some other wonderful people, during this part of my life in Bristol and I would love to share them with you. Geoff Bracey's father John, is such a gentleman and a person that I have a lot of respect for. He is a very hard working man of honour and he certainly guided me, in setting my moral compass. Teresa, his wife has a broad, Bristol accent and is truly an honest talking woman, a wonderful mother and human being. She is absolutely adored by her three sons Geoff, Chris and James who are the ultimate characters of life and express themselves freely, they are a great family. One time, Teresa had the police showing up at her house, telling her that one of her boys, Chris, was racing down the road really fast on his motorbike and needed to be careful. "That's not possible, he has a moped." They ended up arguing, as she stood strong for her son, believing that he only had a moped and not a motorbike. But unbeknown to her, Chris actually did have a bike, secretly tucked away in one of the barns on a farm. For show and to please his mum, he would leave the house on his moped and drive to the barn, swap over to the motorbike and go and have some fun! When it was time for him to return home, he'd go back to the barn and carefully drive his moped home. He had been tricking his mum for some time!

'The Supercar Club', P1 International, provides members with access to all of the latest prestige and performance cars from Ferrari, Lamborghini, McLaren, Aston Martin, Bentley and Porsche in return for an annual membership fee. I was a member and loved the pure luxury to have some fun in a car, of my choice. On this particular occasion, I collected a yellow Murcielago Lamborghini. As I was on my way up to visit Carla, driving on the M1 towards Sheffield, I noticed a Vauxhall Cavalier come up behind me, with little red and blue flashing lights on the front, trying to get my attention, as if to say "I'm watching you." I was doing the national speed limit of 70mph, which is the rightful pace required by Law but suddenly I saw a clear stretch of road with no cars in front of me, as far as my eyes could see. For a moment, I wondered if I should drop down gears and floor the car as fast as I can. I couldn't help myself, I did just that! I left the car behind me, in a cloud of dust. Now, from my own personal knowledge, the Law states speeding is an offence, if it is measured between certain distances but if you return to the lawful pace, then no speeding offence can be detected. This has changed with modern day technology of cameras and monitors, so I don't suggest you try this! I was chuckling to myself, as I returned to the national speed limit. Naturally, the car comes back up behind me and gives me another flash, of his shiny coloured lights, as if to say "Behave yourself." As you have now gathered, being cheeky is part of my personality so…a bit further along, I notice another clearing of the road with no vehicles ahead. Just as I was thinking this, I looked in the rear view mirror and noticed in exactly the same moment, that he had dropped down his gear, ready to take me on but I laughed and waited until he had to put it back into a higher gear and then I floored it! For the second time, I left him for dust and I was doing up to 160 mph!

I then dropped the speed, so they could not record me and for the third time, he came up close behind me but this time he flashed the lights, for me to pull over onto the hard shoulder. I like to listen to the Law, so I followed his request and pulled over.

If the Police pull you over because they think you are speeding, they can either give you a verbal warning, give you a Fixed Penalty Notice or they will tell you that you will be ordered to go to court and you'll be sent a letter telling you what to do next.

He walked over to my Lamborghini and tapped on the glass and indicated for me to wind down the window. Well, I couldn't be bothered to wind the window down and on this Lamborghini, the doors lift upwards like 'wings' hence the name Murcielago, which is Spanish for 'bat' and it's way more fun! So, with a cheeky smile on my face, I got out of the car.

Man: "You're a very naughty boy, aren't you?"

Me: "I don't know what you are talking about."

Man: "How fast were you going, just then?"

Me: "I dunno officer, about 70mph, I think."

Man: "Yes, I know you were doing 70mph but when you floored it and disappeared, how fast did you go then?"

Me: "Probably just a little bit over 70mph."

Man: "Look, if I was going to book you, then I would have done it by now. In truth, I just wanted to see the car for myself, what's it like to drive?"

Me: "Well, when you're driving at 70mph it's like making love to your wife and it feels so nice but when you hit the pedal floor, it's like suddenly turning her over and sticking it up her arse. You know you shouldn't but you just have to try it!" (Apologies to all the women present, who have taken any offence in reading these words but its male banter!)

He was hysterical with laughter and asked me if I could take him to the next junction, just so he could experience the feeling. "Okay, hop in" I said. We got back onto the motorway doing the appropriate speed and then the officer said "Go on, floor it! I exclaimed, "But you can do me with hard evidence!" With excitement he said "I would have nicked you by now, go on do it!" So, at the officer's request, I floored it one last time and I hit around 180mph and then returned back down to 70mph. "My son is gonna die when I tell him about this! He has always loved the Lamborghini's. I have never seen inside one, let alone sit in one but I can go back and tell him about it today. Thank you so much, for an amazing experience!" When he was getting out of the car, he said "Please drive carefully, I can see that you drive incredibly well." I told him "I don't just have a general driver's license, I also have an advanced license for Ultimate Control. "Just take it easy and thanks" he repeated.

With that, the Police left me to continue my journey up to Sheffield and I remained at 70mph, for the remainder of my travels because of the honourable policeman.

A huge lesson in life is how to respect oneself and others. As we have seen over many decades, this is lacking in our humanity as we are programmed like robots. Whenever I have had any confrontations with the Police, in the UK, I have the confidence to say "You must understand that I pay your wages and your wages mean you are here to uphold the Law and not be the Law."

It's like looking at your reflection in a mirror, if you go into a situation aggressive and cocky, then this is the reflection and behaviour that will be mimicked back to you. I can be cheeky in my behaviour but I add the fun side to it and it returns back to me over and over again.

Bristol had so many memories but it was time for me to move on again. I said goodbye to Bristol and was ready to embrace whatever God had planned for me next.

Guy Kelland

Friends Geoff Bracey, Paul Ambrose and Ian Atkinson

Waterskiing   Age 28

Lamborghini Murcialago

— CHAPTER 10 —
SINGAPORE SLING

Spain, was calling my name and so, I returned to timeshares but the industry had changed so much, since my time away from it all. Miraflores resort is owned by Ole Sigurdsson and I got to know him very well, he is such a gentleman and a lovely person to be around. Here, I shared some wild times with Paul Duff, Roy Buck, Paul Porter and Dave Stronach. The administration partners were Sarah Wattam and Marcia McEwan. We made some big money back then and even though I was back doing what I enjoyed, something inside me had changed too.

After a few years of living in Spain, I was getting fed up but unsure why I felt like this because it was not something that I could put my finger on.

Max Beach Bar was one of my regular bars and it was owned by a lovely Belgium couple who had a dog called Max!

Bullying is something that I will not tolerate because of the beatings that I got, as a child growing up. I would not allow anyone to bully me, ever again and no one did try to boss me around, until one day at work, a man who was a lot bigger than me in size, was having a go at me about his girlfriend. No, I was not trying to chat her up but what I did do was call her out because she was one of the managers and I approached her, as I believed there was some deception going on. She then went and told her boyfriend what I said to her, so then, he confronted me and before I knew it, I was nose to nose with him, as he tried to threaten me, I said to him "Just make sure that your first shot is fucking good because that's the last shot you'll ever have on me!" When you stand up to a bully, it's amazing how fast they back down. Now the truth is, that my backside was having a different conversation with me but I didn't show him my fear, as I was actually shitting myself inside! If he had punched me, I would have gone down like a sack of spuds! Since that moment, I have zero tolerance for bullies and I have no fear of death since Lee passed over.

Bullying has become 'normal' in our modern times and it is NOT acceptable to bully anyone or be bullied. They just want to shame you, mock you or blame you and if you allow them, to overpower you, then you will lose your power. Learning to stand your ground, in situations where you feel ungrounded, put clear boundaries around you, so that you are comfortable with what you will tolerate and not tolerate, from the various people in your life. Your invincibility exists in you, it never left you but only you, can find it again and use it to defend and protect yourself and your loved ones.

One morning, Dawson contacted me about a woman he knew and she was under a lot of stress and he wondered if I could let her stay with me for a few days. "Of course!" I said. This lady had been looking after her husband for a number of years and sadly, he was in a vegetative state, through a particular illness. I decided we should go out for lunch and then sit on the beach on Saturday. We sat there chatting for hours, about everything and our lives and as the sun was setting, she turned to me and said "This has been the best Saturday that I have had for years. It has been absolutely beautiful, thank you. It's such a shame that we cannot do this again tomorrow." The next thing I knew, I was on the phone to my partners and just said to them "It's over, I'm done! I have something more important to do tomorrow and I don't want to be doing this work anymore." That was it! I gave up my job there and then, in that exact moment and it felt brilliant! It felt the right thing to do. The next day, we both went out for lunch again and chatted all day on the beach. The intimacy was in her soul and nothing more. The next day, she returned home to her husband and I never saw her again but she had changed my life completely, as I had now retired from work! It only lasted for seven days though! Dwaine Hill, who was previously one of my fiercest competitors in timeshares, made contact with me "I hear you have retired, Charlie." "Yes, I am glad to be out of it," I told him. "We have a proposition for you. We would like you to come to Singapore, to train our people with your knowledge and expertise, it would be extremely valuable here." "Make me an offer!" as curiosity crept in. They offered me an amount that I could not possibly refuse. They flew me over, with my accommodation sorted and my work paid for, for the coming six months as a consultant and trainer.

In this market place, I was learning how different cultures and people had very alternative ways of working in business and how you can make deals with them. When I was selling to the Chinese and the Indian people, they had their own individual styles of devising deals with others. The English and Australian people have a similar way in making deals with others, which I find easier. It's about being smart in business, to understand people and where they come from, so you are able to use your assorted skills to achieve good results, this is what makes good business. The Chinese in general, wish for a 'win-win' situation, for both parties involved. They want to know what you will gain and what they will gain from the trade, as this leaves everything transparent and open, obviously depending on who you are as an individual and if you are authentic. If they are happy with the conversation, then they will buy from you, that simple. The Indian people wish to understand the theory behind the deal, then they will discuss it further with whom they trust, as fellow friends and family. Again, that simple.

Leisure Group Marketing, was the company I was now working for and our offices were in Tower B based in Ngee Ann City. I was training up to thirty people in groups and also working with individuals. The art of selling is mainly to do with body language and psychology and learning how to understand what people are actually saying, with their actions and reactions.

Singapore, is a city-state in Southeast Asia and has been voted the 'best city' in the world to live in, with its security, convenience of life, perfect climate, goods and services, education, medicine, opportunities and its cleanliness and it certainly held up to its name! When I stepped off the plane, my first reaction upon arrival to Singapore, was how warm and humid it was and the colour green was everywhere, as it's a tropical rainforest.

In the beginning, I had temporary accommodation and was told where to meet the guys for a drink, so I followed the directions given to me and I walked from the corner of Orchard Road and Scotts Road to Orchard

Towers. Now, for those who know Orchard Towers, you are probably chuckling as you read this but for the ones that have never heard of this place, I shall enlighten you. It's known locally, as an entertainment complex famously described as the "Four Floors of Whores". During the daylight hours, it is a normal shopping centre and at night-time, it turns into a completely different place with bars, pool tables, with male and female sex workers. With the four floors, the higher up you go up, the bigger the difference you will see and it certainly was a very interesting place to visit, especially for my first night out!

Next door, there is an Irish bar named Muddy Murphy's, which became our early meet up for drinks, before the evening's entertainment.

I did manage to find a place to live comfortably, in a building that stands twenty storeys high. I was in a three bedroomed, penthouse apartment in The Legend, which was situated on Bukit Timah Road. I rented a condo from the Prince of Johor Bahru in Malaysia.. This suite was a place for one of his wives, a former Miss Singapore, who was extremely pleasant when we met up to sign the rental agreement documentation. My neighbour was someone whom I became good friends with but I never knew the truth of his work, until we parted company in Singapore. I later found out that he was actually working for the United States Secret Service but his card of employment showed, that he was in charge of Homeland Security! We are friends even to this day and he certainly shares some extremely valuable information with me.

Singaporean multi-culture, is regarded as controlled and orderly which does have its positives and negatives. The authorities know everything that you do all of the time, as they wish to assure maintenance of their unique way of life and for everyone to live in harmony, together. You are tracked in your daily movements and even two decades ago, you would have had full access to 'Apps' as a service, which in present times we attribute to this technology such as 'Uber' and similar types of companies. So, if you want a taxi, they find where you are for pick-up, via your mobile phone App. They were, way ahead of the times!

If you want a great atmosphere that is guaranteed, the place to visit is on a waterfront stretch that is lined with bars and nightclubs. My favourite ones are the Clark Quay and the Boat Quay. Here you would witness breath-taking water views and vibrant nightlife scenes. All of the expatriates that lived there, got on very well together and because of the circles that I was mixing in, I got to know some people from the banking world. One particular gentleman got a bonus and he decided to rent out the penthouse suite, at the Fullerton Hotel. We were all invited and had a great party there, which lasted for three days! It was brilliant fun, from what I can remember! I was pretty hard-core back then!

For leisure, I would play golf at Sentosa Island, home to various events, themed attractions, award-winning spas, lush rainforests, golden sandy beaches and resort-style hotels. I truly appreciated the exclusivity of my experiences. Great golfers and friends were Reggie Wanchop, Steve Lever, Gary Morris and Kevin Lally. We all had links to China and Hong Kong which were close by for us, to do business in. For years people have asked me the same question "How do you get connected to these people, Charlie?" I have always given the same response "Like-minded people, attract each other!" When you travel from place to place, venue to venue, enter social circles and gatherings, you end up mixing with friends of friends, making new friends, who have the same interests in life. You have to weigh up the positives and the negatives and remove the negatives, from around you and surround yourself with others that make you feel positive and see the good in you, support you and love you, for you being who you are. Remove the negative people who are close by, that feel less about you, than you do. There are no tricks. There is only truth.

I loved it when my children came to visit! Carla was at Bath University working through her Sports Science Degree, when she came over to visit me one time and I took her over the bridge to Johor Bahru, in Malaysia. The only way to get there from Singapore, is by using the Johor-Singapore Causeway, it serves as a road and rail link, as well as a water pipeline between the two countries, where you have to pass through customs. In those days, you could get DVD's incredibly cheaply and as Carla was a student and had little spending money, she wanted to stock up on some films, so I took her to a large supermarket and we purchased up to nearly 200 DVD's! We arrived at customs and were threatened for arrest! We were there for about an hour, as they looked through the films and discussed the matter at hand, as I explained to them that my daughter was visiting me from England and she simply was a student, wanting to take home her film supply. The only concern they had was "Are you going to sell them in Singapore?" The answer was, no! So thankfully, there were no arrests that day!

Dwaine was a character! As well as having a business with timeshares, he owned a vineyard and distillery for whisky in Tasmania, Australia. Within five years, he had acclaimed the 'Gold Star' recognition on his wines, which just said it all, about his personality! He knew how to get the best out of things and he never created an average wine. In the Ngee Ann City building, you would find shops like Louis Vuitton, Coco Chanel, Gucci, Jimmy Choo, etc and Dwaine would showcase his magnificent wines for the public and I would love the cheese and wine events, where he would introduce various models and new designs with flair. Naturally, when you are invited regularly to these events, you meet other people and mix with an array of personalities, which in turn creates these endless social circles.

Six months had now passed and I had completed my work that was requested of me and then Brian Lunt, phoned me from his resort 'Absolute' on the island of Phuket, Thailand. He wondered if I could go and help him with the same job that I had just completed. I was willing to consider his proposition and he came back with a great offer, which I accepted.

I began packing my things to explore the magic of Thailand.

Ole Sigurdsson, owner of Miraflores

The Singapore Lads

Ngee Ann City

Johor Singapore Causeway

CHAPTER 11

Sawadee Krap

I was getting ready to repeat the same programme, as a consultant and trainer in Thailand, which is known beautifully, as the 'Land of Smiles'. As soon as I arrived, I was required to acquire a work permit, which would be organised for me by the Thai Mafia. Everybody works with the Mafia. These rules are very simple 'If you work for them, you are safe. If you do not, then you are not safe.' They are completely open and transparently clear. It actually works! Life is easy and things just get done. There is no bureaucracy or 'red tape'. Everything just gets done, even though these rules are old fashioned, from the perspective of our modern age. It has the 'old school' elements with the simplicity, of respect and honour and it keeps the streets clean, tidy and safe, with a managed operation that is uniquely controlled.

Before I continue my story, I will take you down memory lane…but first, if you get the opportunity to speak to any female, that may have lived in the East End of London during the hard times, please ask them "Are the streets more safe today, than when you were growing up, when the Kray Twins were running the show?" You may suddenly retract yourself, to what I just stated. "How could you support the Kray Twins, Charlie?" But I did not claim to support them but I do wish for you, to open your mind and process your thoughts further. I have mentioned before, about keeping hold of the positive and getting rid of the negative in your life. The Kray Twins, founded the infamous gang known as 'The Firm' and they were labelled as criminals of organised crime and Yes, I can see where all of the darkness may have exploded into sheer evil, as murder, arson, assaults, control, etc. But I can also see the light that surrounded them in their fight, to look after their community, against the authorities and for a better cause. The balance has to be found somewhere in 'between'. Maybe they lost that balance somewhere along the way? There has been so much corruption in the world, where it can get lost on a manufactured idea, upon certain individuals or as gangs, to deflect that the crime is from the government itself and that the evil manifestoes, in a different inhumane way.

I used to know Freddie Foreman personally, as he owned a club in Marbella called "Eagles" and I used to frequent it and play snooker with Freddie. He was extremely kind and generous to me but also a man, I knew not to cross. There was one time, when I had left Banana Beach having listened to the famous Mel Williams, who had a wonderful setup on Sundays with live music on the beach and as I headed over to Eagles, I realised I had either lost my wallet or someone had stolen it and when I arrived, Freddie asked me if I wanted a drink and I said "No, not until I have won some money on the snooker table!" as I was a hustler. He instantly gave me ten thousand pesetas, so I was 'liquid'. I thanked him very much! And when I told the lads during the week, they said "Wow! Do you know who he is?"

I said "Yes, he owns Eagles!"

They said "No, do you know who he is?"

I said "I play snooker with him at his club, Eagles."

They said "No, he is the Kray twins Henchmen!!!!"

I said "No! I had no idea!"

I made sure I arrived early the following Sunday to pay him back! To me, he was lovely and I never had any reason to be scared of him.

In Thailand, my base was in Kamala, where I lived in a large detached house. I loved the beauty of the local people and their community spirit. For leisure time, me and the lads would go 'Go Karting' to release any pent up feelings and to clear our heads. There were two tracks, which were virtually opposite each other, one was for the tourists and the other one, was the fast one where we could go flat out racing and have a real blow out! It was such an adrenaline rush and brilliant fun!

During my time in Phuket, I met singer, songwriter Bill Padley, in the Burasari Hotel at the Floyd's Brasserie, which was run by Keith Floyd, one of the world's greatest TV chefs. All three of us became good friends and I certainly would recommend the dining experience!

Brian Lunt was a Liverpudlian, born and bred and he certainly was an 'ideas man', that is because each day, he would come up with around five new business ventures. One of the ideas usually sounded like a good plan to put into action, the other four were usually, not so good. But believe it or not, some of the not so good ideas paid off and earned him a fortune! One idea, was to create a sexy timeshare resort on Bangla Road, which is a well-known street that is simply geared up for sex! His hotel 'Bangla Suites' oozed sexual energy everywhere, the rooms were luxurious with sexy materials in the bedding, carpets and curtains, the colours were sexy, the ambience was sexy…it was simply, sexy. On the top of the building, on the roof, you could go for a swim in the pool and make a grand entrance by helicopter, if you so wished, as there was a landing pad for guests! On the ground level, the reception space opens up, to an exquisitely designed water feature.

Brian, also managed the 'Sea Pearl', which was located at Patong, in Phuket on the seafront. But I cannot express the depth of sadness, at the loss of lives that occurred here, from the Tsunami, 26th December 2004 at 7:59am local time. It was triggered by an undersea earthquake, making it the third most powerful quake ever recorded, with up to 280,000 people having been killed by the water, with hundreds of thousands of others displaced.

My memory of the people is the spirit and soul of the community. The resilience of the citizens, having to create some kind of 'new normal', is indescribable. Since this tragedy, the authorities have put in place early warning systems but no one that lives in this region, listens to the threat because they look to the animals and not the 'false' alarm. This is because when the Tsunami hit, all of the animals had followed their instincts and left lower land to go to the hills and now if the people hear the sound of the early warning alarm, they look to the animals, for reassurance and if they are still in the streets, then everyone will continue their day as normal.

A man that worked for us, shared his memory from that tragic day. When he saw the giant wave coming in land, he rushed to his motorcycle so he could speed away, as fast as he could but it was so close to him, that the water was physically touching the back of his bike and when he reached the hill, he jumped off his bike, onto the safety of the land and with his adrenaline, sheer terror and relief of being safe, he lost all control of his bowel movements. If he had not got away, in in that precise moment, he would have been dragged into the sea and lost his life. He broke down and wept with the knowing that he had survived, he had just touched death. The lives lost and complete devastation, was international news.

Brian, owned other resorts based in Pattaya, Koh Samui and in Beijing, China and I would travel to each of these destinations, during my stay in Thailand. Angela Meir, was his business administrator and Frank (Philip Mason), was the General Manager of the resorts. He now owns a new one, called Twin Sands Resort.

Beijing is a massive city and during one of my business trips, I was invited to the China World Hotel and I had the privilege of meeting, the Chandon family, who are the lineage of the world class brand, Moët & Chandon and their visit, was to introduce Champagne to the Chinese market. At that time, the Chandon grandfather was in the top five 'Grand' Master of Wine, which is a type of qualification that is generally regarded in the wine industry, as the highest standard of professional knowledge. There are five levels of being a connoisseur, all of these levels include the understanding of the whole construction and the creation of wine, with professional experience in the field.

1. The starting level is an estimated 5,000,000 around the globe.

2. The second level is an estimated 200,000 worldwide with 5 years' experience.

3. The third level is an estimated 10,000 worldwide with up to 20 years' experience.

4. The fourth level is an estimated 100 worldwide of 30 years' experience.

5. The fifth level is an estimated 5 worldwide as the 'Grand' Master of Wine with 40+ years' experience and the ultimate connoisseur.

During this evening event, he did not speak but his grandson spoke on his behalf and with every word spoken, it was passed down from his grandfather where you could see the immense pride written all over his face. It was far more receptive for the Chinese to listen to these words from a young man, rather than an older gentleman. The elders in China drink Sake, which is a rice wine that has been their 'tipple' for generations, so the best audience to attract the 'new' idea of champagne to, was the generation of young adults. The launch of the evening was a set-up, for selling the idea that champagne is the best choice of drink, when you go out socialising. An ice cube was developed, which was made out of synthetic materials that you could freeze, which had flashing lights on the inside and changed colour, which meant that, for every bottle of champagne you purchased, you would receive a flashing light ice cube, as it would arrive at your table in a see through bucket. This became a fun game! It would then become competitive. So, if you bought two bottles of champagne, you got two flashing light ice cubes and maybe the table next to you, may want to have more flashing lights than you have! It was a gimmick that had a huge impact on the sales of champagne. I decided to bring some ice cubes to the UK but needless to say, the spirit of fun was completely lost, with questions similar to "Is it biodegradable or eco-friendly?" This was the typical British response! No humour, fun, games or role playing for a business notion. This was my expectation, knowing they would lose out on a great business plan that was initially and fundamentally, a fun thing to do. You can't make these things up! Where's the fun in life? You are meant to grab the idea, try it out and then if it's a success, you can look at creating eco-friendly materials for the ice cube. Why squash a notion that could be a win-win situation, for all the parties involved?!

I travelled around Beijing in taxis and generally ensured I had two post it notes with me, one in English and one in Chinese. The information written down could be, my work address or home address or whichever destination I wished to go to. I would also have questions written down because no one spoke English. On a few occasions, out of curiosity and for fun, I would ask the driver when we went around Tiananmen Square, the note that said either "What happened here?" or "Can you tell me the history of Tiananmen Square, please?" Their reactions would be, sudden silence, a hand going over their mouth or even using the 'zip' motion across their lips and I did get a few looks of disgust! The Chinese have been told not to speak of the mass killing that occurred on 4th June 1989. I did hope someone would have opened their heart and shared their experiences with me, about themselves and their beliefs but it was not meant to be.

Once again, my work was complete and I was humbled by my experiences. My thoughts were to return to Marbella, Spain but Lee needed my help with his business. So, I booked my flight to Alicante, where he was now based.

The Land of Smiles

Freddie Foreman owner of 'Eagles'

Bill Padley

Keith Floyd's Brasserie

— CHAPTER 12 —
STOCKS *AND* SHARES

Lee was arrested in Bristol, during his late teens, as he was caught with a large quantity of money and drugs but somehow, he had managed to escape and get to the airport, where he phoned me up and said "Dad, I need to get out of the UK, urgently! Can I come and live with you or do I have to go somewhere else?" "I will look after you son, come and live with me in Spain." I didn't know the details of this urgent situation until he landed in Spain and told me what had happened and I was just happy that he was safe with me, at my home. He did keep a low profile, so as not to get the attention of the Police and he settled down and began working for a financial institute broker's network, where he learned the trade of being a broker. He started to make good money, with what he had learnt but he was also intuitive and listened to his sixth sense, which helped him make good deals. Investing in stocks and shares, can be a risk but Lee's business had gone big and he was making large amounts of money, in a very short space of time and because of his success in shares, in the Alternative Investment Market (AIM), he became a magnet and people would want him, to do business with.

Launching a product on the market and issuing shares, the individual truly believes that their merchandise is the one idea that will make them millions and millions but the truth is, few actually do make their dreams and visions come true. The high moments are extremely high and equally the low moments are even lower. You have to be of a strong constitution to be in the stock market world, where you knowingly, will have to participate with direct financial chaos. It's like being high on adrenaline, all day long and then you crash for a time, whether that's a break for sleeping or to reboot your mind and body or the alternative is to shut down with an addiction that gets you through the days. In this industry there can be depression, bipolar, Attention Deficit Disorder, Attention Seeking Disorder and even suicide.

When the profits are in danger, investors can get nervous but if you can gain someone's fortune, they will return to you, for more business. If you lose somebody's fortune, they will not return for any deals with you and the word may even get around. So, there is no benefit in losing money, only to make the money. I can give you an example of 'penny' shares which are usually, very small companies that are yet to establish themselves. You can buy a share, for as little as 1p and if the shares go up to 50p, you have an increase in the value. So, if you had originally put in £1, you would have £50 back, £1,000 in, you would have £50K back and so on.

A 'boiler room boy' is a term used in this commercial enterprise of brokers and this term can be categorised as illegal dealings, from the salesperson cold-calling to potential investors, from a 'room' but it is sold publicly. They will convince customers to buy a product that will bring a huge return and only the buyer can decide if it is a scam or fraudulent, for what you personally create on the market. It is your moral compass that you adhere to, to whatever outcome you desire. Naturally, there can be greed and the darker end of the spectrum. You play how you want to play and it usually ends up as Karma. You get out of it, what you put into it.

Lee worked with his close friends, Andy Quinton and Liam Ryan and with their secretary, Ingrid Katy DaSilva. I have complete admiration for their work ethics, unbelievably hard working and they were always above and beyond the call of duty and that's, what paid off! They were always first in the office and the last to leave, sometimes they would not even come home to sleep. Alas, along with this came the party life and I did understand this way of living, with the women, champagne and cocaine! This is where I left Spain and travelled to Singapore and Thailand.

I came back to Alicante, to help him to improve things with his drug, alcohol and women issues, as he was truly overwhelmed and needed support. I was here, at his request but after time was passing, into months and months, I could see from an outside perspective, that I was not helping him in any way, which I thought I was. His issues extended and they got worse because now, he had me in the office and took things for granted. He was crazy but I loved Lee so much, who as my firstborn, had taught me how to love from the heart. His journey was a roller coaster, exhilarating and scary all at the same time. He was 27 years old and had done more in those years than others might have done, over a few lifetimes!

Lee, finally realised he had a major cocaine problem and with Liam and Andy's guidance checked himself into South Beach Baptist Hospital in Miami, which is regarded as one of the best in the world for addictions with the highest success rate at 18%. He was desperate to get clean and he did find it extremely difficult, being locked in this facility. I used to fly out regularly every 7-10 days for a visit, to support him and be there for him during those three months that he was in rehab. I was only allowed to see him for one hour each visit, so to pass the time, I ended up hiring different Harley Davidsons from EagleRider, Miami, and did the same one hundred mile trip from South Beach Miami to Key Largo to Key West, just for some pleasure and a beautiful ride and to make sense of life. Lee did get a bit better and he came back to Spain and started dating his secretary Katy, as she was known. He did eventually slip back into his previous lifestyle, with work, money and drugs.

Because of my travels and business, I became a Zug resident in Switzerland, even though I lived in Spain. Some people have said that I made this choice for tax evasion but I did not, it was legal avoidance and it is within the law, which clearly states that 'evasion' is illegal but 'avoidance' is completely legal. I had this residency in Zug for a decade and had been approached and encouraged, by the Mayor of Marbella, Jesus Gill, (this was before he got himself into some trouble with the authorities) with the advice of keeping my residency away from Spain, as the system was extremely corrupt, which meant that I could remain living in Spain. I was introduced to a lawyer named Thierry Tissot to help me, with all the legalities and to complete the legitimacy of this change. I purchased a property in Zug where I spent many wonderful times there, looking out onto the Lake Zug and feeling so much gratitude for the luxury of such beauty and magnificence.

I had the honour of meeting HH Prince Rashid at a charity event. He was not from Dubai but a UAE resident, he was a citizen of his country of origin Pakistan, and he had business in Dubai. He invited me to join him in Dubai and we got to know each other and became great friends.

Little did I know, when I had my home in Los Flamingos, Marbella, Spain, that my neighbour and now good friend, was an honourable, kind gentleman and a high profile UAE businessman, Mr Rashid Al Habtoor!

I now knew two Rashid's in Dubai!

Lee, Carla and Charlie

My 7 bedroomed house

The cars

Rashid Al Habtoor Me and Thomas Kramer,
who built Star Island in Miami.

— CHAPTER 13 —

DELIGHTS OF DOWNTOWN DUBAI

Joe McGrath, was someone I was linked with, from the Bristol days, his company did the morning travel and weather daily updates, for GWR Radio station in Bristol. To myself and other friends, he is fondly nicknamed 'the fridge' and this is because one evening, James Canon, Joe and myself had been out drinking and it will come as no surprise to you, that we were drunk! Joe was hungry, so he grabbed a chair, opened the refrigerator door, plonked the chair in front of the open door, sat down and proceeded to devour the complete contents of the fridge, hence the title! He quit the radio show, after many years of broadcasting and left Bristol to pursue his business in Dubai, where he time-lapses records of the construction of buildings, so that three years of work is condensed into six minutes! The projects exhibit the construction of a building, beginning with the foundation and building up to the top as a complete full structure. It is phenomenal to watch this happen!

Before I go and visit any country, I always ensure to learn the correct etiquette, to know what is acceptable behaviour or unacceptable behaviour and I will memorise how I should present myself, in professional and personal interactions because I respect the cultures of others. In Dubai, I was told that I must not stare at a woman, wearing a Burka but one time when I was out walking around the malls with Rashid, I accidentally looked at some beautiful eyes, they were magnetising and then she winked at me! I turned to Rashid "Oy, she's just winked at me!" His reply was "They can wink at you but you cannot wink at them!" In England, we call this 'double standards!

Rashid was always generous in his time, when he would show me the delights of Dubai. He loved to show off the wonders and beauty of his country. When he realised what work I was involved in, he told me that I would be able to help many of his friends. He knew of the 'deep state' and its satanic systems that exist, which is basically stealing your personal ownership of possessions and materials. "You have to be aware of the truth and play them at their own game." He clearly understood the depth of corruption and whilst I was in the Middle East, I connected with many, many more families. All by association of introductions, social circles and being authentic. The Middle East dominion, is managed by a handful of families and the ones that I had the pleasure of meeting in person, were all good people. You get to know them by default.

I have a special friend in Dubai, who has been researching, for over forty years, high level global corruption and how real money, should be backed by Gold. As an analyst and a visionary, he regularly writes in-depth reports, offering advice on strategies in wealth protection. This has almost driven him to bankruptcy because 'they' have tried unsuccessfully, to stop him making this factual information, public. Now that we have arrived, to the current exposures regarding the activation, of a global Gold backed Quantum Financial System and the potential adoption of NESARA and GESARA, he says to me "Is it really happening? It's hard to believe!" He has accurately forecast, the 'Reset' in the world economy, currency and banking systems for many decades.

Sheikh Marwan, is the eldest son of Sheikh Mohammed and is one of the most humble and beautiful human beings, that I have had the pleasure of meeting in my life, people can put expectations on Royal families and their opinions and judgements, which some of it can be true but many wealthy people are generous and compassionate, as it depends who you are as a person and not how much money you have.

Suhail Al Zarooni, is the Crown Prince of Pakistan and truly an adorable man. I learned so much about business and acquaintances in a dining experience! That is how they manage their deals, by sitting together before discussing anything. In the West, they tend to meet at a restaurant and sit down to eat and discuss business matters at the table but in the East, food comes first. You all gather around delectable delights of food, that is set out magnificently and you enjoy the feast! During this time, you cannot disguise your natural manner in how you eat and what you eat, if you share your food or eat alone, etc. You learn a lot from people, when it comes to eating in company!

The Grosvenor House Hotel, was my base in Dubai and expatriate's stayed here because of The Marina, which is a development with all of the amenities close by. It had its own bars, clubs, restaurants and leisure facilities, so naturally it's a practical place to stay. Even though it is a hotel, they have other options, including three bedroom apartments and I did use these condos, if I was doing business with people from Iran, Iraq, Syria, Libya and other places. Their name would go under the title of 'Persona non grata' and my procedure, would be for me to book an apartment in the hotel, then leave an envelope with a room key inside and the room number with the concierge and give them instructions, to give the envelope to Mr... They would bring the people straight up in the lift, to the apartment and our meetings could last up to four days, we remained inside and enjoyed room service and did not venture outdoors, so to keep all of our discussions in private. This was for their own personal protection because of their concerns that the Cabal may know where they could be and yes, they probably did know their whereabouts or location. Most of the men that I had dealings with in person, were honourable and they simply wanted to look after their families but the politics was against them because of the dishonesty of the federal agencies and bureaus, who destabilise the people. They are such beautiful people with passions and love of their cultures but we have otherwise been misinformed about these countries and places because of the mainstream media. Obviously, you have to be careful and wise because of Embargo, this is the government stopping trading to control you and create limitations and restrictions and I have never stepped outside of these boundaries, as it is illegal and punishable. An outsider does have the power, to force and change this regime with stronger influences and the predominance similar to Donald Trump, who is the 45th and current president, of the United States of America. Choosing peace and unity to align with each other and work together in harmony, all in the cause for the highest good of each individual and the greater good for them all.

When I was in the African continent, I became aware of the amount of money that changed hands to guarantee elections, to have the desired outcome. Simply put, certain leaders would pump money into the other countries, to make sure that they got the right leader in power, no matter the cost. This continent is very much tribal and if you offered 'X' amount of currency to a tribal leader, he can make sure that his 'tribe', will vote for the person that you specifically want, to have as a leader and I saw this exposed in Africa, India, Pakistan and a number of other places around the world.

How certain 'things' happen, in the correct order and in the correct manner. Again, I was just Charlie the postman, organizing and planning from A to B as it was government to government and I can assure you, that they will arrange personal and private custom clearance. It moves under Diplomatic Immunity, which ensures the people are aware of the movement, get consent from the Federal Reserve and have permission granted with documentation, to completely satisfy the custom diplomats that have the authority to move the dollar. This technically is a Law that the USD belongs to the United States, so even though it is going from Africa to Dubai and it's not going near the US, it still belongs to the US and that is why you need their consent, in these large volumes of cash. Truly fascinating details, facts and truth of our reality that is hidden from the general public. If I was not there to experience any of this, then I would never have known about the hidden agendas.

The maximum amount of money that you can 'lift' on an aircraft by Law, is 400,000,000 which is four metric tonnes, which is four cubic metres in one hundred dollar bills and all rather convenient, as the math makes it all very easy. I did find out that the CIA was using huge cargo planes and transported billions, which was totally illegal! We had to operate within the 'laws' because the Law states, four hundred million is the maximum that can be covered by insurance, whilst mid-air on the plane. You cannot exceed the value of the plane, even an Antonev An-225 costs less than some of these planes and it could carry 250 tonnes, which legally, you were not allowed to do that but because it had taken off from a military base, in one country and landed in another military base, in another country, there wasn't the customs restraints that you and I would generally have. You can land in a military base, without any customs issues at all. The CIA managed to move huge amounts of cash for drugs, paedophilia, and human and sex trafficking and anything else that is unimaginable. You would be able to take off, from a US air base in America and land in a US military base, anywhere around the world, without any interrogation of customs and I can tell you, that there has been some thought process already in place, to close down these military bases worldwide for that simple reason, of being ports of entry and exit.

One thing Britain will know of, if you do the research, that a young lad was knocked off his bike, by a diplomat's wife and she managed to 'hop' onto a plane and leave the country, without having to justify herself or to be questioned by a judge or with any simple apology of her action, to support the deceased. Isn't it shocking to know that it depends 'who' you are or connected to, that you can arrive at an air base in the UK and once you are enclosed in that military area, you are regarded as being in a military zone and 'safe'. Technically, you are in a piece of America even if you are in England because it is categorised, as being on 'American soil'. The British authority has no authority whatsoever in these foreign bases, as it is managed by their own military force, police force, etc.

Dubai, became the base of my business because of the amount of clientele that was there for the taking, which was unbelievable, to connect with people from all over the world, that were getting blocked by the Cabal, just for moving their own money, as the deep state's only intention, is to steal it from you. I had a court case that lasted for five years and it all began because I was arrested in London! I was waiting to make a pick up from somebody, who owed me money and they were ready to pay their debt off, we had made the arrangements to meet for collection but what I did not realise was, he was actually under surveillance, for the movement of alcohol for cash and this had nothing to do with me at all but I was there, in the wrong place at the wrong time. It is not illegal, for me to collect my own money in cash that someone owes me and I was determined to win this, in the courts and eventually, I did win my case! But the British government stole my money and kept the wealth, as they claimed there was a 'technicality'. I am once again highlighting the corruption, which is priceless and Karma is a wonderful thing! I know I will see justice for the people because I have all the time in the world, to see it exposed in the mainstream media over the coming days, weeks, months and years.

My residency in Zug, Switzerland lasted for about ten years, where I changed it to the residency in Dubai. Every ten days or thereabouts, I would travel between both bases, of this country and Spain, as I was busy picking up currencies from Russia, China, Africa and even Europe. Because of my social personality, the respect that I have for others and my general manner of listening to people and wanting to understand them, this always opened up great opportunities for me. It never took me long, to find the 'top man' at Customs or in the Criminal Investigation Departments (CID). I was always upfront explaining what I did and who I did it for. This makes life very simple, when all is clear from the start. The CID, along with Customs would register me into their systems, as a person that has the authority to carry funds and I always ensured that I asked them which documentation they would require, to satisfy them and to verify who I was. As an example they may say to me "We need to know, which bank account this money came from." But the money may not have come from any account whatsoever because the individual did not trust the 'system'. And so, my documents would satisfy them.

Did you know that you are only insured for £75,000, if your bank or building society goes bankrupt? Most people do not know this. The 'bulk' of cash is never stored in the banks, it's kept outside, in various places. It does not matter, if you have thousands or millions of pounds, you would only receive compensation of £75K, if they go bankrupt. Hence, when you have this knowledge and the cash, you would naturally want to move your money out of the bank and have various options to choose from, like putting your money into positive alternatives such as gold, silver or platinum, etc. This is much safer to do, when you understand the corruption at play, by the companies you sadly have been misled, to trust. I recently had a conversation with one of the Heads of Customs in Spain, I told him "Next year, 50% of the banks will go bankrupt in Spain." He questioned me "What about my money and pensions and all that I have put away for my future?" "If it's under £75,000, you have nothing to fear" I shared with him. He was shocked by this and I do hope he looked for better options. I personally do not have a pension because I do not trust 'them' and your money can disappear, overnight. Lately, I have discovered that the Police force in Spain, have lost their pension funds, it has all disappeared! This presently is being kept under wraps, even though many Police have walked away from their positions of service.

The MSM have blamed this on King Juan Carlos, for running away to another country and stealing it! This is a complete lie, to cover up their own theft and I have no respect for thieves, do you? I ensure that I know the system, to then follow the system, where I conform with the 'rules' and the 'law' of their manufactured corrupt system, to cover myself to the best of my ability but they can easily turn into slippery snakes and the sliminess of horrible people. Simply put, evil at work and play…like a devil in disguise.

In Dubai, there is a company Jetex, that has their own private terminal and it is the most magnificent and stunning terminal in the world! The owner and C.E.O is Adel Mardini and his right hand man is Ossama, who manages the terminal. I became great friends with Ossama, with my openness and my work and as trusted friends, he introduced me to the private Customs department, where I met with Farooq and Mohammed from the Customs and CID departments. This was so they knew of me and my business and it was to keep everything straightforward and open and do things their way.

Honesty is simplicity.

Because I used to work with certain members of some powerful families in The Middle East, Farooq would ask me "Why are you using these people?" "Why do you ask me that?" I questioned back. He told me "My family can offer you better service. Instead of using them you can use us." And he continued to share more details. In this arena, it's intelligent to find the safest and best value for a money deal. If you can offer me a better deal, even by 0.5%, then I will be talking to you. All pretty simple really. Do your homework. Be transparent.

With my life being so busy, I did need looking after and Marie Fe, was the one who was doing just that.

Joe 'the fridge' McGrath

Charlie, Rehan Merchant and Marcus Thesleff

Charlie

Charlie and Khalaf Ahmad Al Habtoor

Suhail Al Zarooni

Charlie and Sultan Shar Ansari

— CHAPTER 14 —
LOOKING *AFTER* CHARLIE

Whilst I was in Singapore, my friend Gary Morris, suggested that I should get a live-in maid "You need looking after, Charlie. You're a single guy and busy working all of the hour's god sends. You need a clean house, laundered clothes and good meals." And then he told me he knew of someone.

I was introduced to a young Filipino lady, called Marie Fe Juliano. I had seen her CV before her arrival and she seemed a good person and pleasant in character. It was a 'yes' straight away and she moved in with me, that same day to start looking after me. This was my first ever experience, of having a live-in maid who was not a girlfriend or a wife, she was just employed to take care of me and my home. My house was always clean, clothes pressed and food on the table, she truly was an asset to me. Marie Fe, was also companionship, if there were times I was home after being out all day and she was someone to talk with. I was happily single and had been for a number of years and had no thoughts of a romantic relationship with her. Her nickname was Fe and this is what I called her, 'Fe' I would call out whenever I needed something. I introduced her to a local Filipino family, where she could spend time with her own kind and socialise, as she was committed to me seven days of the week. I felt it was positive for her, to be with others and have time away from work.

When I was moving away from Singapore, I asked Fe if she would join me in Thailand, to continue her employment as my maid and thankfully she said yes! My house was in Kamala, Phuket which was situated between Patong and the airport.

Kamala is quite famous for visiting 'Phuket FantaSea Show' which is a cultural theatre 'Las Vegas' style show. It's an elephant show which is absolutely amazing to see and is certainly entertaining. The animals do not perform as a circus act, they just play a part of the cast and it also boasts to have the largest buffet in the world that seats about 3000 people, for exceptional Thai and international cuisine

When I was ready to leave Thailand and move back to Spain, I asked Marie Fe if she wanted to come with me back to Europe, she said yes. She came back to Alicante first and then Marbella.

My friends used to mock me with Fe. As I lounged on my sofa watching sports on the television, I would shout for her "Fe" to get some snacks or top our drinks up, the guys would echo out "Fe" "Fe" "Fe". I started to get embarrassed, that my friends were taking the piss each time I called out for Fe, to do something for me. I had an idea! I would get her a 'buzzer' so that I did not have to shout out for her, but 'buzz' her. It worked! I would press the buzzer and she would immediately arrive "Sir, what do you want?" And whatever I wanted, she did it and Fe always looked after me, incredibly well and all of my friends thought she was wonderful. Fe was deeply religious and on Sundays, her day off, she would go to the Church and socialise in San Pedro, outside of Marbella. These days, I would tend to feel sorry for myself, having a heavy hangover from the previous night's entertainment and now I have to look after myself, without my maid!

Whilst I was in Spain, I suggested to my son Lee to get a maid like Fe, so he could be taken care of too. He agreed to this and I asked Fe, if she knew of somebody who would be interested in the vacancy and yes, she did. Edna was then employed by Lee but sadly her work was not as diligent and she had managed to wash Lee's passport on a few occasions, as she did not check his pockets before putting them into the washing machine! The passport office told Lee that if it happened again, they would refuse him another passport. He certainly did give Edna a stern chat about it! Edna stayed working for Lee, until he was killed in a car accident. I felt guilty for Edna having no money or employment, so for some random reason I said to her "Why not come and work for me, Edna? I have a seven bedroomed house and you can be company for Fe and both of you can share the workload and I will pay you the same money as Lee paid you." So, here I had two maids looking after me full time and this encouraged me to have more parties, to create more work for them and so my life became one big party!

Robbie was introduced to me, by Edna. She knew of him from Church and he used to clean my cars and do odd jobs around the house. The next thing I knew, I had all three of them living with me! I did offer Robbie a place to stay but I told him that I would only pay him, when he did a job that I required from him and so he agreed to the deal. A little relationship blossomed between Robbie and Fe that I was unaware of and then out of the blue, Fe was pregnant! Nine months later, a baby arrived and now I have four people living with me! I named this sweet little girl 'loopy loo' and as she grew up and started speaking, she would call me by my name, Charlie but Fe, Edna and Robbie always called me 'Sir'. Not that I had ever asked them to call me Sir, it was just their way and they worked for me for years.

At one stage, Fe wanted to go and visit her family in the Philippines but she was unable to because her residency had expired. I chatted with my lawyer and he suggested that the only other option would be for her to marry someone in Spain, only if she was in agreement to this. He told me to see which friend of mine would take on the responsibility and as I wanted the best for her and not for her to be in a situation, where she may get mistreated or disrespected. Well, I had no plans for marriage, as I loved my single lifestyle and my intention was to remain this way! I never believed that I would ever marry again and as our current situation worked well, with us all living together, I thought if I marry her for the papers to be legal within the eyes of the Law, then this was the answer to the problem. I was told by officials that I would have to go for an interview in Malaga to make sure that all was in order and correct. I told Fe right from the start, that I was willing to look after her, to make sure that she was okay but I would not put her in my will, nor would I wish to consummate the marriage.

But I did wish to give her a gift as a token of our agreement and I purchased a very nice ring for her to keep, no matter the situation, so that she would always have something.

For the coming months, we spent lots of time discussing her family's history and dates of birth, etc. as we did not know what questions they would ask us, on the day of the appointment. I knew her very well because of all of the years she had worked for me but I wanted to be informed of things that I had not known previously, to reassure the officials during the interview. When the day arrived, we both walked into the office, sat down and looked at the woman opposite to us and she gave us both a brief look and continued to sign the papers and hand them over to us, she did not ask one single question!

Me: "I was expecting a lot of questions."

Lady: "I don't need to ask any questions, you both walked in not holding hands."

Me: "What does that tell you?"

Lady: "It tells me everything! I can also see the ring on her finger."(Implying the expense)

Me: "Okay, thank you."

Lady: "And you both look very happy."

Me: "I am happy."

Fe: "I am very, very happy too."

Lady: "Off you go now, good day."

So, off we went into the room, where we had our civil ceremony and they gave us our official papers, to declare our marriage to each other. I felt that I had done the proper thing for Fe and now she could travel to visit her family and show them the new family addition, little loopy loo!

I was out on a date one evening a few months after the 'wedding', when a lady questioned me!

Lady: "I thought you were married?!"

Me: "I am. This is my girlfriend."

Lady: "Where's your wife?"

Me: "My wife's at home looking after the baby and she knows I'm out with my girlfriend."

At that moment, she was enraged and went mental at me! Naturally, she did not know the whole story of our arrangement.

Me: "My wife knows my girlfriend and my girlfriend knows my wife and they don't have a problem with it!"

I spotted the lady's husband, who was laughing at the scene that had been caused by his wife, because he *did* know the full story.

Gary Morris

Edna & Marie Fe Juliano

— CHAPTER 15 —
TURKISH DELIGHT!

Nursel Akifova Feizulova, was born in Turkey, Istanbul. At the age of 4, her parents chose to uproot themselves as a family unit and move over to Varna in Bulgaria, as the work was much easier to find, with her father being a shipbuilder by trade and wanting a better way of life for them all and for Nursel's education. At that time, Bulgaria was one of the nations to the east of Europe that was still under 'The Iron Curtain' which is a reminder to the people that their country is within political boundaries, as a communist and capitalist state. This country did not have any respect for the Turkish people and when Nursel reached the age of 8, she had her passport taken from her and replaced with a Bulgarian passport and a new name, Nina Akifova. This occurred in the 1980's.

From a young age, Nursel trained as a gymnast and represented Bulgaria for ten years and over the coming decade her passion for being on the stage was expressed travelling around the globe in the 'Show Business' world of Circus and Cabaret, with eccentric and magical experiences combined!

One evening, I went out with one of my friends Simon Bold, to my regular fashionable restaurant and bar 'Pravda', which was owned by Simon, Pravda is the Russian word for truth. Desiree, who worked with Simon, they were also in the midst of dating each other and I was invited along to a wine tasting night that they were holding at the restaurant. There, I met three women and only knew one of them and not the other two. Naturally, I introduced myself but I could not remember her name! I kept asking her throughout the night, to repeat it for me. "Nursel" "Nursel" "Nursel" she would politely reply each time. I think she was getting fed up with me but it was such an unusual name and I also had had a few vodka and red bulls! When I asked her if she would like a drink from the bar, she refused. I noticed she was not drinking alcohol or smoking cigarettes and I am wondering to myself "Why is she here at a wine tasting event and not drinking anything alcoholic!" I was intrigued by her and found out through her friends, that they had brought her out for some entertainment, as she was always extremely busy with work and a young child, she had a son, Justin, who was 2 years old. I wanted to get to know her but she wanted me to piss off! I realised that she just wanted to be out with her friends and not have me pestering her for a date or another relationship as she was trying to get out of one, not get into another one! I could not help myself though, I had to get to know this woman.

Me: "Let's go out for dinner?"

Nursel: "No."

Me: "What about lunch?"

Nursel: "No."

Me: "How about breakfast?"

Nursel: "No!"

Me: "We've got to do something! I leave for Miami in four days!"

Nursel: "What are you going to Miami for?"

Me: "A stag party, a hen party and a wedding with my friends Luke and Caroline."

Nursel: "Enjoy your trip and no way! will I go out with you before you go to Miami. Okay, if you remember me when you get back, I'll consider it."

Me: "I'll be back in ten days and I'll give you a call."

So, off I went to Miami but did not come back for a month! I came back much later than I anticipated but it was worth staying for, as I had such an amazing and memorable time with friends. It was now January and I decided to make contact with Nursel, for that date. "No!" was the reply but I did not stop there. In the end, she agreed that we could go on a date, as long as Simon and Desiree joined us at Pravda. I agreed and we arranged a date and all that I can say is, on that evening we just clicked! There was something special about this woman, that I had not experienced before and when the evening was coming to an end, I gave her the common goodnight kiss cheek to cheek but as I passed by her lips, I gave her a cheeky peck!

Nursel: "You're cheeky!"

Me: "I can live with that! Let's do this again sometime?"

Nursel: "Yes, I would like that."

Me: "Maybe just the two of us?"

Nursel: "I'm happy with that."

So we agreed to do the same thing, at the same restaurant but without Simon and Desiree. We had such a lovely time together on that date and halfway through I looked at her and said "You know what girl, you're the one!"

Nursel: "You don't even know me."

Me: "You'll find out, don't worry about it."

No one had ever caught my eye and heart, the way she had.

I have slept with many women and had many 24hour relationships, but I had never found anything that I wanted or anybody, that I got close to loving again. Nursel had all the magical qualities and more, and my heart fluttered! So, we went out together on a few more dates, to different places and we got on great together and on the fifth date, halfway through the meal, she stopped eating her food and looked me in the eye "I will tell you something. I share my house, I share my car, I share my food, I share everything but I do not share my man. If you are ever unfaithful to me, never ever come and say that you are sorry to me, just leave."

Wow! That hit me hard. I had never been told that before in my life and it really impacted me, it was a massive wake up call to realize that I cherished somebody that was valuable to me and true. We dated for about six months, before I asked her to move into my home with me, "Are you for real?!" she said. I knew that we would not know what life would be like living together, as a family but I just wanted to be with her "I love being with you and I love Justin and he loves me and I want to look after you both." It took another four months for Nursel to come round to the idea and terms of my offering and now that she had processed it, we moved in together exactly nine months after we had met. The chemistry between myself and Justin was also brilliant and as any single mother can appreciate, that if their child or children have a positive and loving connection with the man they love, then it is a bonus, when they become a family unit.

On the morning of our Christmas Day celebrations, we were playing games together in the lounge.

Justin: "Daddy."

Me: "Yes."

Justin: "Can I call you daddy?"

Me: "Of course you can, you are my son."

He ran straight over to me and gave me a huge hug and from that day until this day, he calls me daddy. I don't buy into the political narrative of 'step-son', I feel this downgrades him and I won't do that to my son. It is far more to nurture, than leave to nature. I am incredibly proud of my precious little man! Lee, my eldest son can never be replaced but it helps with the pain inside. Justin has so much positive and vibrant energy, he would have loved him as a brother.

When Nursel moved in with me, her mother joined us too and at that time, I still had my three staff and loopy loo. I now had an army of staff that I did not require anymore but I did have a certain loyalty to them and now my house was full!

As Nursel and her mother did more and more in the house, the other three staff, were doing less and less. Life had changed for us all and so with that, they went one by one. First Robbie, then Edna and then Fe. There were some rocky moments during this transition but it was well navigated, as there were some bad feelings, but that's life and it does move on!

Life was getting better and better all the time with Nursel and Justin but I knew she really wanted something, that she had never had before and that was to be married! Because of how I felt about her in my heart, I knew it was time to take this next step forward. I decided to ask her father, so I wrote in Turkish, Bulgarian and English (because I do not speak Turkish or Bulgarian and he did not speak English) with my request. I found the right moment to ask her father to give me permission, to ask for his daughter's hand in marriage, which he graciously accepted.

I knew nothing about diamonds only that they sparkled! But I did have a friend, who does know about gemstones. So, I asked them for a specific type of diamond that I had heard about and with that, I designed the ring myself and I had it specially made with the stone mounted. The day the ring arrived, I was so excited! It looked better than I had, ever expected. My plan was to propose to Nursel on the beach, as the sun was going down that evening but because she knew me so well and we understood each other's ways, I was struggling to contain my emotions.

Nursel: "What's up with you today?"

Me: "Nothing."

Nursel: "I know you, you are up to something!"

Me: "Don't worry, you'll find out all in good time."

Nursel: "No, you do not hide anything from me."

Me: "I am not!"

Nursel: "You are! I can tell the way you are acting. There is no need to hide anything from me."

Me: "This time there is!"

I am not good with hiding things at all and I gave the game away completely. I am so transparent and cannot lie and so my emotions got the better of me.

After an hour of her poking me in the kitchen, typically she got me to tell her everything and I had to propose to her in that moment. "Yes!" she said immediately with amazement and then added "Why didn't you wait until this evening, to ask me to marry you?" I rolled my eyes as tears popped out, it was a magical feeling and I had emotions that I had never experienced before and all because of Nursel. I now know what true love is, with a woman by my side, her love for me is unbelievable. Women are like a mirror and the more you put into them, the more you will get out of them.

If you give her food, she will give you a meal.

If you give her a house, she will give you a home.

If you give her sperm, she will give you a child.

If you give her shit, expect tons back!

The same goes for your children, it has nothing to do with money. It's about time, care, appreciation, attention to detail and most importantly, love. I do joke about her but I do say it with seriousness. She is 95% perfect and 5% terrorist, when she goes off on one…take cover! We always know when she is cross with Justin, the English turns to Turkish and the volume goes up and with that tone of voice, even I get scared! But she is everything I have ever wanted in a woman plus 50% more, I am truly blessed!

Ikbalya, her mother or Anya as everyone calls her (Turkish for Mum), is an amazing woman who does not speak any English and I can only speak the simple basics in Turkish so, with the language barrier she can't tell me off! But I do get 'the look' every now and then, just so she can let me know that she does not approve of me at that moment.

She never takes sides between us, even when Nursel and I have had a row over something. Her Muslim faith is still valued and I did join her one time whilst she was doing Ramadan, which is a religious month of fasting, prayer, reflection and community and I chose to do this to support her, understand the experience and lose some weight! I did make it through but in the second year that I tried to join, Nursel ended it for me because I was getting so grumpy!

Nursel has been my rock through some difficult times. I had been a single man for such a long time and it took me awhile to accept certain things and adjust to our family life, which has taught me many things including, patience and compassion. People also think that being in the money business means that you would not have financial setbacks but this is untrue. Things can and do go wrong and the buck can stop right there. On a few occasions, I have had to honour payments when something has gone wrong and I have even had people steal money from me and with that, I am left with the debt to repay it in full, to the original party involved. You learn the hard way and it brings you back into reality!

I do wish to share a special story with you.

Prince Rashid invited us over to Dubai for a visit, as he wanted to see me regarding business and to meet Nursel. We were picked up and taken to a hotel and had the pleasure of staying in the Presidential Suite as guests. We checked ourselves in, unpacked our belongings and settled into the splendour of it all and as I was waiting for Nursel to get ready, and as she wanted to look perfect for meeting a Prince, she was taking a long time to look immaculate but I was getting bored and a cheeky idea popped into my head! So, I hid behind the chaise longue. Nursel was now ready and called out to me "Charlie" but she couldn't find me anywhere. I keep silent. She starts to search the rooms, under the bed, looking in the wardrobes, going into the toilet and even out onto the patio and we are on the top of a building! Her only next option is the front door and she sees that the keys are still in the dish and the door remains locked "Charlie!" then suddenly she notices the curtains are shuddering, as that was me in fits of laughter. "What are you doing, Charlie?" "I was playing hide and seek for some fun!" I teased. My intention was to loosen her up as she was petrified at meeting Prince Rashid and it certainly relaxed the situation with laughter. She was so nervous because she did not know what to expect, when he would arrive in the room, well, it's not every day you meet a Regal Prince! Even though we were friends and business associates, the behaviour with women is different and it could go in any direction of greeting one in various manners or no greeting at all!

Then there is a knock at the door and I open it to see Rashid, with his entourage of a dozen military men. He walks up to me and embraces me with a big hug. I introduced Nursel and he walked over to her and gave her a big hug too but her arms were rigid by her side, as she was unsure how to respond! After the warm welcome, we discussed some more business and then our meeting was over.

On another trip to Dubai, I contacted Sultan Shar Ansari, to see if he could help me with finding a place for beauty treatments for Nursel. He said he knew just the person for her and he would get in touch with them, to see when they would be available. I put the phone down and not much longer after that, Shar called me back to say everything is organised and can I ask Nursel to be at the front door in thirty minutes and he will take her there to the venue himself. I was very grateful at this offer and so Nursel did go downstairs and when she reached the front door, a Rolls Royce Phantom was waiting for her and she was grateful! This is all very normal in their everyday lifestyle.

I decided a couple of years ago, to introduce Nursel and Justin, to my father.

When we arrived at his home, we were not allowed to go into the house, we had to just stay in the garden. The house being off limits because of his faith and mixing with 'others' outside of his religion, is not a position the Plymouth Brethren wish to put themselves in.

We stood talking for a time and he was quiet in his manner and polite. He did say "If you want something to eat, we will make it for you but you know we cannot eat with you." This was not unexpected.

When we had arranged this meeting beforehand, I asked my father, if he could mention this visit to my three sisters, Phillipa Pricilla and Rachel, as it would be lovely to see them again after 30 years. Phillipa and Rachel turned up, which was strange because the last time I saw them, they were turning into their 20's and then looking at them at age 50! I am sure they thought the same of me because I have changed a lot. We had lost our emotional connection as family a long time ago but it was a pleasant moment, to see them all again. Even though there is a detachment between us now, I still love my father. Life took us on different pathways and I wish them nothing but peace, love and happiness.

When we were leaving, Justin approached my father and sisters to give them a hug, as this comes second nature to him but they told him "We can't do that I'm afraid." Justin was completely baffled!

I still wake up each morning and look at Nursel and fall madly in love with her all over again, she is such a beautiful soul. So many women say to me "How did you find her? What was it about her?" My response is always the same "She has the X factor, I cannot explain it with one answer, as its millions of things!" I have changed dramatically in these nine years and not because she wanted to change me but because I wanted to change me. She needs me for support and love and this reminds me of my responsibilities, in life. Nursel fills my void, with a beautiful package of love.

Our wedding ceremony was in Barbados, a magical experience and you are invited to join us in the Caribbean, on the next page.

Desiree and Simon

Nursel, Charlie and Justin
move in together

Nursel and Charlie Early Days

Nursel, Ikbalya and Justin

Engagement ring

Nursel having Gymnastic Fun

Circus lift

Before the show

Showtime

— CHAPTER 16 —
My Caribbean Queen

20th February 2016 is the date we chose for our wedding.

Now, it was time to get the plans prepared and organised, to create the most perfect day to remember. We decided very early on, not to marry in Spain where our home setting is because we know so many people and that meant, we would have to have an enormous setting, to allow a vast number of people to celebrate with us and in fact, we only wanted our dear family and special friends, to be a part of this sacred ceremony. Our desire was to find that dream destination for us both and Barbados hit the spot and was the one place that neither of us had ever visited before during our travels around the world and so the Caribbean, appealed to us both, as the location to become man and wife!

We took a flight out, to the famed Platinum West Coast to see what would be on offer for us, to create our dream experience. Nursel did not only want to marry someone she loved dearly but that it also had to be the perfect setting on the beach! We organised most of the details through various options that were available and ensured that all of the arrangements were seamless. We organised the whole wedding with Wendy Kidd, Debbie Parris along with Astral Macalesher-Griffith and Joan, who was the housekeeper of Holder's House, which is an exquisite 17th century house, built on a former sugar plantation. Which is currently home to the Kidd family and has been for over four decades. Jack Kidd is a dear friend of mine.

When we arrived in Barbados and checked into Sandy Lane Hotel, at the last minute, they told us that it was now not possible for us to get married on Sandy Lane beach because they were unexpectedly, much too busy. I looked at my wife-to-be and her whole face dropped, with complete shock and disappointment at such news, as everything had been fully arranged prior to our arrival and we were so close, to the day of our wedding. They offered us another option, which was to rent out Landmark Cottage for the week, which had its own private beach and was situated directly next door to the Hotel itself. This was a good alternative, to have our ceremony on the beach and the pre-reception in the garden area.

And with literally a few days to go until we would make our vows to each other...Nursel's face started to swell up and panic set in! She had an abscess in her gum and was struggling to speak and was in pain. This was the wedding of her dreams and now a more serious set-back! We spoke with Cecily Spooner, who was in charge of our wedding plans and she assured us that they had a brilliant dental practitioner, who was not too far away and she would contact him immediately. We were willing to pay any amount of money to cover his time, if he was having to come out of his usual business hours. The arrangements were made and we travelled to the dentist surgery clinic and then waited for him to arrive. He certainly was eye catching, as we saw him drive up towards the clinic, mounted on his Harley Davidson with blonde dreadlocks!

He was a Bajan, which is a term used to describe the Barbados citizens that are still in connection to their descendants, like a cultural identity worn with pride and honour. He was an adorable gentleman and through the appointment with x-rays and checking her mouth, he reassured Nursel "You'll be perfect, count on me, I will have you right for your wedding day!" Her concerns were put to ease and she was feeling happier. He turned to me and said "You like my Harley Davidson?" I told him that I loved them! He then told me that, each year there was a great ride around the island with these bikes and tomorrow, by ship, there were about one hundred cruiser bikes coming over for this event. "If you wish to join us for the day, I have a spare motorcycle and it will be perfect, 'A Fat Boy' for you to drive." Wow! What a wonderful offer but as I was there to be married, I declined the opportunity but maybe one day, we could travel back to Barbados for our Anniversary celebration and I could enjoy the experience then! Thankfully, after a day, Nursel's mouth began to heal, the swelling, pain and inflammation had reduced, so she felt confident all would be well on the day.

I had rented out all of the properties, for all of our guests, to ensure everyone was looked after, for this occasion. We had gatherings in the day and parties in the evenings. I loved the grand piano, out on the Colonial House patio, where many songs were sung. I have many talented friends from the musical world. Simon Giles is a pianist. Stefan Booth is a singer and actor and Linda and Dani Newman from the group Masquerade, whom I asked to be our wedding singers.

Other people who were there to enjoy the delights were Glenn, my son and Carla, my daughter. Simon and Desiree, if you remember, Nursel wished them to join us on our first date. Dawson, my godfather and his wife Fiona who is also my godmother and my good friend Stuart Tidy with his wife Vanessa, who originally introduced me to Jack Kidd plus a lot more, sixty five, to be precise.

The day came for us to become man and wife!

I was getting myself ready to commit to Nursel, my heart was blooming with pride. Justin and Stefan's son, Benjamin were our Paige boys and his daughter Tabitha, as the little flower girl.

When I was waiting at the altar with my back turned to the guests and looking directly at the sea, I waited for Nursel to walk down the aisle to join me in our union ship of love. As the music began, I was ready to turn round to see her come towards me, with her father by her side. I had feelings that I had never experienced before, as I saw Nursel's face light up, as her dream had come true! There are no words that can convey the depth of my love and gratitude that my heart felt in that exact moment and she looked exquisite and radiantly, graceful. We were giving each other our hearts in that special time and I was so humble, to have our loved ones to share it with us. God has given me a beautiful gift and I am honoured to call her my wife.

The whole wedding was unbelievably good fun, from beginning to end. Such an incredible atmosphere and to see my wife bursting with happiness and joy is etched into my soul.

There were some speeches made in the English tradition, by my two best men and my Godfather, Dawson and I said my gratitude speech, also. There are no speeches in their tradition, in Turkey and Bulgaria and Nursel stated that her father would never speak in public, as it was not his style, so we were extremely surprised when Harry, Nursel's Father stood up to say some words in his native language and it was translated for us all, by his grandson Dennis, this was a very special moment and it was a beautiful surprise to hear what he had to say, "Charlie's a big man with a big heart and we love him." How beautiful to see Nursel's face light up, with these unexpected surprises!

Carla, my daughter can be an entertainer in her own right! She chose her moment to sing me a song, just for her daddy! It was a sentimental moment between us. She said this song reminded her of me "Like a Prayer" by Madonna and she sang it from the heart and I felt extremely warm inside.

For the remainder of the time, after the ceremony, we stayed in Sandy Lane Hotel and everyone else, remained in the properties by the beach and in Holders House.

The amazing people of Barbados, have a wonderful culture. I loved it when we had rain and when it does, it's a tropical downpour! And the local folk who are in their cars, will stop to offer lifts to random strangers in the street and ask them where they can take them! How wonderful is this! We did the same in our hired vehicle and our car was full! I just wanted to join in with the spirit of the togetherness that they share. Such a lovely way of life and community connection.

In Sandy Lane 'The Green Monkey Bar' is intriguing. You are not welcome to take your mobile phone or any recording equipment into this area and you are advised to leave it, in a safe place. What happens in there, stays in that place and does not venture out into the public. The type of people that enter here, do know what is going on in the world in different realities and I certainly heard some fascinating stories and it is where gentlemen go and talk about life. It is a discreet and private bar for the world's elite and I do believe, it has even been named as the 'Den of Iniquity' but I call it a 'Cave of Wisdom', full of positive energy and knowledge.

On the worldwide, famous golf course, I noticed a wealthy gentleman playing by himself and his caddie, was the very well-known Bajan open Champion, for the last six years but was a caddie, for this multi billionaire! Fascinating!

I have to mention though, that through the magnificence of the day, there was a huge void, not having Lee by my side. He would have been very proud of his father. I know he is happy for me, I feel it in my heart.

Nursel and Charlie

Charlie, Simon and Stevie G

Glenn and Carla

Justin, Tabitha and Benjamin

All 65 guests

Taking our vows

CHAPTER 17

THE WARD BLOODLINE

April 4th 2009, 9.00pm.

It was a beautiful evening and I was enjoying the company of friends in Portside, one of my regular bars, when my phone rang and I took the call, it was Carla.

I was pissed and telling the lads 'Look it's my daughter, my daughter's ringing me!".

She had just received a call from Glenn and was relaying the message back to me.

Carla said, "Dad, you're pissed, listen! Fucking listen to me!"

I was joking about, "She's telling me off again, she always tells me off!"

Carla spoke with urgency "DAD, FUCKING LISTEN TO ME!". I listened to her words... "There's been an accident, I need to talk to you!" she said. I moved away from the lads, to hear more. "There's been an accident, I don't know what's going on but you need to get up there! It's on the golf course, near Lee's!"

I could tell by the tone of her voice, that something was wrong and suddenly I knew exactly where Lee was, like a sixth sense. I have never moved so fast in my life and jumped into my car and raced to him! I came across a roadblock, which was about half a mile away from the location of the accident, it's a private road from the back of the Hotel. I was stopped by a Policeman and I was trying to tell him that I believed my son was in the accident and he had a white Lamborghini. I wanted to know if this was the car in the accident. As I stood there, a blacked out undertaker's van drove straight past me. My emotions, as you can imagine, were in all directions with the sheer horror of the situation and feeling numb and shocked, all at the same time. With the language barrier between us, he could only confirm that the car was in this accident and the only thing that came to mind was to phone Sylvia, my Lawyer based in Malaga. In general, she would never answer the phone after 6pm because she spends that time with her family but she suddenly picked up the phone and I was telling her the situation and could she help me to translate the officer's words. When he passed the phone back to me, she delivered the news of Lee's death! She shared the words with such kindness, consideration and compassion, for it to sink in and keep me calm and grounded, with the utter shock to my broken heart. Earlier, when I arrived at the scene, I heard a noise that will remain with me for the rest of my life...I was shaken by a scream, which had an ear-piercing shriek, from nearly half a mile away, it was Gonzalo, Lee's friend and driver, who was identifying Lee's body at the scene of the accident, he was completely devastated.

Finally, the officer allowed me through but I had to stand back, whilst they recovered my boy's body. The Chief of Police approached me and suggested I go home immediately, to make the necessary calls to Lee's loved ones, to let them know what has happened. He assured me, he would come to my home in a few hours, as he gently put his arm around me for comfort.

I went home fragmented, in my mind, body and soul and I had to phone Lucy, his mother, to tell her that her first born son was dead. I also made the call to Katy, so she could tell my 18 month old grandson, Alexandro that his daddy had gone to God. Many more calls were made worldwide, to deliver this heart wrenching news, including my father, as I wanted him to be at the funeral for me, as this one time, I needed his support and he assured me he would be there.

The Chief of Police, did knock on my door at midnight and when I opened it, he held out his arm in front of me with a bag of cocaine and €30,000 and with all of Lee's possessions. He gave all of the items to me and I took them from him and then he stepped forward, put his arms around me and hugged me. He was a father who understood me, as a man and saw the bigger picture, rather than turning up with an arrest because of the drugs and the money. This was such an honour and my respect for him, will always be in my memory and heart because of that, poignant moment.

Lee had been driving his car and showing off to a mate who was a Royal Marine and someone that he had met during rehab. The car had come off the road and gone over the edge and had landed 200 feet down, just short of the golf course, on the riverbed. Lee was pronounced dead at the accident and the lad was taken to hospital, with a suspected broken spine but his injuries were not major and he was able to attend the funeral, a few days later.

In Spain, the funeral is generally 48hours later. With the preparations being made, I asked my best friend Steven, to stand by my side as I was ready to see Lee's body in the morgue, by the cemetery. My first reaction was to look at his hair because it did not look like him, as the people had flattened his hair and brushed it over to the side, like an older man. "You can't bury him like that, he was fussy about his hair, I'll give you some pictures to do his hair right, as you're not going to bury him like that!" Steve said "What? Only you would notice something like that." I told him "I can't send him home, looking like that." Lee was proud of his looks and he loved styling it, in a spikey fashion.

I wanted an open coffin for the funeral, where two hundred people attended to say their goodbye's to Lee. My father never turned up, to support me and this reminded me of the tattoo on my arm, a dagger going through the heart. It finally gave me closure and it made me realise that I never would want or need anything from him, again. When you reach a place of such deep emotional pain, something cracks open and it disperses with acceptance. I did learn later on, that he was persuaded by the elders not to attend. I expect nothing from him or wish for him to change his ways, it was all meant to be, I can see that now, with an open heart.

At the wake, I wanted pictures of Lee, showing his face as he laughed and was having good times, reminding us all of the funny things he did that made us smile.   I wanted the memories to be about the positives and not focus on the negatives. I buried all of his naughty antics, as I did not want to be consumed by the pain because I am extremely proud of him, no matter what he did. It was so wonderful to hear so many new stories about Lee, from so many different people, that wanted to celebrate him.

This was the most traumatic period of my life and I was surprised, how strong it made me and how it stood me in good stead, to take responsibility for myself. I was all alone, with no support and overtime, me and Carla seemed to be there for each other, when one was weak, the other was strong and vice versa. Grief evolves over time and the heart grows stronger, if you allow it to. It's a private and personal journey that has to be honoured and we can connect with our loved ones, in our own way.

Let's go back in time to see my children growing up, which will take us to the present day, of what I hold dear to my heart.

Lee, my first born son, was hyperactive as a child. He had so much energy and we were always flat out with him. We did ask for advice and we were told that Tartrazine could be attributing to his behaviour. Tartrazine is an artificial additive put into food and liquid as a yellow dye, which makes things more pleasing to the eye, for the consumer to buy commercial foods, such as marmalade, cordials, crisp, cheese, sweets, ice-cream, etc. So, we changed his entire diet, to more natural foods and he calmed right down but he was still active and restless and was always getting into trouble at school, with other problems that were getting more difficult. I would get calls, to say he had escaped and was missing from school but we always found Lee. There were times, I even gave a kid a tenner, to tell me where he was hiding!

Lucy and I separated and it was not getting any easier, for Lee over the years. He went off the rails and finally, he was expelled and put into another school, Thomas Moor Boarding School in Dartmouth, for children with similar disorders but he was still getting into trouble there. By this point, Lucy could not cope and the decision was made, to put Lee into foster care. Prior to this, he had been man of the house after I had left the family, when he was aged 4 and even though we did see each other, as regularly as I could, he had taken on a big role, for such a small little man. He remained in foster homes, until he was in his teens and when he left school, he got into a bad crowd, with buying and selling drugs.

Lee was incredibly loving and had a lot of love to give to others and he was always funny and making people laugh, he was adventurous and a strong natural leader in life.

Alexandro, his son, is a magical pianist and a credit to him.

Glenn, my second born son, arrived 18 months after Lee. He was such a sweet, peaceful, calm and gentle child and was generally, just a good lad but he too, was having a difficult time at school as he was very clever but just did not like being there. Glenn was the best BMXer that you could find! The tricks that he could master on his bike, was amazing to watch and you could see that he was in his element, doing this. He enjoyed being outdoors, rather than staying in and playing board games. Glenn, is the most loyal and trustworthy person you could have in your life, standing by your side and as you can imagine with the bond that he had with Lee, things got really difficult for him when he was separated from his brother, Glenn took on being man of the house, around the age of eight and he was very protective with looking after his mum, which he still does to this day.

The depth of connection between Glenn and Lee was palpable, the bond was so strong. Even as young children, they loved being together and Glenn even came over to Spain to join his brother, to work with him but when Lee passed over, it was like he had lost his twin soulmate.

He did have a relationship with Verity from Cornwall and together, they had Hugo, my first grandson. He loves the sea and surfing! Hugo, continues the legacy of his BMX biking skills, passed down from his father! Glenn, then married Henrietta from Norway but they separated and I have another grandchild, named 'Baby Lee', whom I adore! He lives in Norway, we speak on occasions and I hope to spend more time with him, in the coming years.

Glenn is such a sensitive soul and I love him dearly.

Carla arrived 18 months, after Glenn was born. Our little girl was special because she was our first girl and she loved being with the boys. From a very young age, she loved playing football, she would bury herself into it and loved it with a passion! She established something deeper, that the boys had not found because she had made a connection to something, where she could express herself and with this, she met like-minded people, that helped bring her to a happy place, with what she loved doing. It certainly helped her manage the difficult times in her life.

She started playing for Newquay Football Club and became very successful and then moved onto Bristol Football Club. In later years, she joined me in Spain, as she had the opportunity to play for the Women's Football Club in Alicante and played for Hercule CF Femerino, as it was formerly known back then. Her friend, Charlotte Nicholson, played for the same team and they had such wonderful experiences. Spanish football training can be slightly different, compared to English football training, I remember when Carla told me, how she was taught, how to take a dive near the penalty box, so that you could get penalties on purpose. In England you are not taught to do this, as it's believed to be playing the game, unfairly.

With Carla's hard work paying off, she played at Sheffield Football Club and to the highest of levels and she even represented England, for the BUSA team, where I watched her play and felt so incredibly proud. She has also managed Sheffield United Ladies and Birmingham City Women F.C., in the English Super League and is now in her own right, a Football Manager. Carla has a beautiful child, named Hartley, a double love from the Heart and the memory of Lee. 'Heart-Lee'! She is my first girl grandchild and at sixteen months old, she is incredibly talented and she can already count to ten and repeat the whole alphabet!

All of my children got on really well together and I do remember a time, when Lee was in boarding school and Glenn, Carla and I went to visit him. They started to play a game of football, with some other kids and by the time you know it, I'm the goalkeeper! It became a fierce and aggressive game, as my kids were very competitive playing against others. When we got home, Glenn and Carla were telling their mum, they had some pain, so Lucy took them to the hospital. Well, that was a good idea because it turned out that Glenn had a fractured ankle and Carla had a fractured wrist! I hadn't even noticed! Lucy gave me a big telling off when she found out.

Justin was two years old when I met him and I had the pleasure of marrying his mother. So now, I have another family and a child that I call my son, who is younger than two of my grandchildren! I remember when he invited me to his nativity play at school, when he was 4 years old. I had never been to one of those, I had only heard about them "Yes, I'll come along, what are you doing in the play?" He told me "I'm the star of the show." I did a little research of the show and I thought "He must be playing baby Jesus!" On the night of the show, he came out on stage, with his little face squeezed into the front of a star! He had the biggest smile, you could wish for and he was so proud, in his moment of glory, which he got to share, with his mummy and his daddy! Justin is so talented and has taught me many things that I did not know of, when I was growing up as a lad. I support his exciting ideas and he has many of them! By age 3, he was pony trekking, then he moved onto Brazilian Jiu Jitsu, then tennis, football, swimming but his first love was dance! He joined a group, with the same passion and they were so good, that they signed up for a spot on 'Spain's Got Talent", as a team performance.

Around the ages of 3-4, Justin would join Pablo, as he was entertaining guests playing the saxophone, at Nikki Beach. They both ended up becoming a double act and they would attract a huge audience, watching their magical rhythm of dance and music, as they flowed together and it was so amazing, to see Justin become another star! Then dance, turned towards gymnastics and his dedication is surmountable. He astounds me, with the repetitions and consistency of getting it perfect! He has asked if he can go to the Olympics! He goes to school 9am until 4pm, Monday to Friday and during the week, he will train an additional fifteen hours, doing gymnastics. On Saturday, he will train for another three hours and on Sunday his day off, he asks me "Can I go to the trampoline park?!"

Carla and Justin are great friends.

Glenn and Justin have a special bond.

Lee and Justin have an indescribable connection because, when I took Justin to the cemetery, where Lee is buried, he would sob uncontrollably and he has never met him! But I do believe they do share the same spirit and they would have loved each other, if they had met.

I have talked about my parents and I have nothing but love for them, to varying degrees and in different ways.

My father is still alive but he is too old, to change his ways, as his programming is ingrained into his entire essence.

My dear mother has now passed over. Glenn told me of her death, six months after she had passed over. No one from the Brethren had told me she had died, my father said he did try to contact me, but I knew otherwise. I was completely devastated! I found a quiet place and sobbed and even though I had not seen her for years because of the forced separation of the religion, this umbilical cord, had now been severed and it was a deep, deep pain that took time to settle, as I digested the news of her death.

And life continues on…

Lee and Alexandro

Glenn, Hugo and Baby Lee

Mummy Carla and Hartley

Justin on Spain's Got Talent

Father and son

CHAPTER 18

MOVING MONEY AROUND

It all began in Spain, when one afternoon, someone asked me "Charlie, I need some Peseta's, where can I get a good deal?" I got them a good deal because our banking system was with The Bank of Credit & Commerce International, in Gibraltar. But this bank in fact, turned out to be a front for a drugs ring gang, who would change their cheques for cash! We did know something wasn't quite right about it all, because the percentage rates were a lot higher than we got from anybody else but we never asked them any questions, we just used them because they were better. When this man asked me to change his money, from Pounds to Pesetas, we had no written contract, it was just a verbal agreement between two people. They would hand me their money and have to trust me, with my side of the arrangement. If they needed documentation, I could give it to them once the transaction has gone through but until they get it back in their hands, it's a gentleman's handshake. The cash business is not about contracts, you basically use the old school rules and be a man of honour. So, I had no training in money, only what I had learned from my family business and then thereafter, with the chickens, employment and self-employment but it became second nature for me, being able to handle money easily. I have always felt comfortable to be around money, the supply is endless around the globe and everybody has access to it but sadly, the 'systems' have us believe otherwise.

Because of television and films people are misled, thinking that when they put money into their banks, it all stays in the bank vaults somewhere inside the building but this is not true. Men and women have been made to believe that their money is safe in the bank or building society. As an example, if I walked into a Lloyds bank on a general high street and showed up with £10-50K, they would shit themselves! They would ask lots of questions and may even panic and/or refuse the money or call for the manager. This is the mentality or should I say the brainwashing, from the Government. I have mentioned to you, that if the bank went bankrupt and you had more than seventy five thousand pounds in your account, then

---

you would lose anything above that amount but in reality, how many of the general public have this amount of money. But if you understand or certainly are willing to ask questions about these systems, then you will uncover much more, than you ever thought could be possible. You may even be shocked at the deceit, which has been going on for decades with the peoples' money, which is you and your money. It is complete corruption hidden by a screen. HM Revenue & Customs (HMRC) are involved in this but pick on the 'small people', the general public which is basically you and your family. The elites, millionaires, famous, royalty and many more, do not use the typical banking systems, which we know of. Let me explain some more, about these words that I am going to add into my story and if you have never heard of them, I would suggest you do your own research on them, in more than one area. They appear 'new age' but these words have been hidden from us and put as conspiracy theories but facts are not theories, they are facts. Here are a few expressions in our society today.

New World Order

Mind control

Deep State

Cabal

The list goes on and on and this is one of the reasons why I wrote this book because I want you to know the truth, so that you can build a better life for yourself, your loved ones and for your future generations. I have obviously experienced my life in money and have been surrounded by certain people and certain situations, to let you know that it is all true and it really does exist and I don't want these lies to be kept hidden anymore. It is time for the corruption to be exposed.

Have you ever looked at a bank note? I mean really looked at a bank note! I don't mean the colour of it or what number is printed on it or even the famous figure on it. Have you ever read the words and tried to understand what the words actually mean to you, as you do use the notes, every day. Whether you believe the Queen has monetary value or not, the bank notes quote 'I promise to pay the bearer'. This means, it is a promissory note. It does not say 'Subject to terms and conditions, laid out by HMRC'. So, in effect the HMRC disrespects the Queen and the Monarchy! They do not care, as they are part of the deep state. They are corporations, protecting other corporations.

Her Majesty's Customs

Her Majesty's Revenue

Her Majesty's Police

Her Majesty's Courts of Law,etc

It is all under the same umbrella and these 'rulers' and authorities keep you, in a fear based way of living your life, under their orders and rigid rules that they want you to comply with. You must obey! But in truth, it is none of their business, where your money comes from or where it goes to. How you use your money or manage your money, is completely up to you. If you are not breaking Common Law, then you are doing nothing illegal but a high percentage of the general public do not, even know about these Laws. We are forced to believe in Maritime Law and this is completely illegal, as you are a human being living on the Land and not of the Seas.

The foundational reason for the pressure, to follow the route of monies, was to do with the drug trade. 'They' want it to be tracked and traced and it's not rocket science, to work out the success rate on closing down the drug trade, is about 4%! If this was a statistic, of any other crime our in society, it would have been left out, a long time ago and not much attention given to it and that's the problem, that it's managed by the government itself, which is actually, the Cabal. So, you have to understand that the tax authorities, police and courts, are all greedy and they want it for themselves.

What people overlook is, the banking system is a corporation, run by the deep state and they are the ones, who actually handle drug and weaponry money, and have done so for decades and decades and decades. Ultimately, they know exactly what they are doing, through the system of finances and it is finally being exposed, in its entirety, in lots of different layers and will continue to do so, for many years to come. Millions of people will be shocked about this and horrified at the falsity, of what their actual rights are, as a human being and how they have been kept in the dark about it all. This is your Government because it is worldwide.

This is how my business evolved from Spain. More and more people wanted to exchange their money with me and the stakes got higher because of the social circles I was attracted and from other connections, so it became natural for me to carry on working for myself. I had learnt the art of the trade, over a few decades and have met the most amazing people and some of the wealthiest families and the seriously rich, who have wanted me to move their money and even to purchase goods, services or property for them. They trust me. I have also moved money for the Government, which is why I know the information, which I am sharing with you. Now, I have been accused of many negative phrases, like 'laundering' or 'tax evasion' but I am an honest business man and I do not lie and I am not dishonest, about my work. I am simply the courier and I move money from A to B. Imagine me, as your postman, I don't ask you what's in your letters or parcels, before I deliver them to you. How do I know what I am handling, when I deliver your items to you? So, yes I may have handled money, that could have come from darker places but I do not know of the details, I am the courier man and the only time I will know the details, is if the receiving bank, has requested additional information in advance. I always notify the receiving bank in advance and they will inform me, of what they require from me.

I do everything that I can, to make sure that I operate within the guidelines and I document each transaction, to satisfy all of the parties involved. I have specific procedures that I follow, to be clear and transparent. When I arrive at the airport, I declare the money that I have in my possession, to keep my back covered. Customs, just want to know that you have made the declaration, they will ask me to present my certificate/documents to them. Now, this is where you may get someone who is purely nosey, just so that they can look at the contents of my luggage because they want to see what a large amount of money actually looks like. I ask them "Yes, you may take a look, only if you have a private room to view the contents." If they haven't got a private room, I may say "I will not open this for the general public, to see the contents and I have my declaration with me." And there's always a dickhead, somewhere along the line! Who feels he needs to boost his ego on the job but I always remain calm and play the game. One man asked me "Where has the money come from?" I replied "I have custody of this money and it is my responsibility." That ends the questioning.

I remember one guy at Customs, he said to me "Aren't you worried about carrying around all of that money?" "Yes, I am! I'm worried about you because no one else in the airport knows that I am carrying this money. Everyone else thinks it's my socks and underwear not half a million quid and now you, know I have it, so you're the only person I need to worry about!"

Another time when I arrived with £500,000 in cash, their counting machine had broken down, so they decided to count it by hand! Which took over two hours to complete. This was because he had lost count, the first time around! So, I did the decent thing and bought them a decent quality counting machine, as I have better things to do than waste unnecessary time with them.

There are times I will use a security guard, from ex-military personnel, as they are highly professional, skilful and discreet, compared to me! People have tried to mug me, that's why I use a security guard. Our procedure would be to meet in a hotel, usually, in a family room with an adjoining door, so we can discuss all of the details in private and then depart for the airport. In movies, you know them as decoys, so if anything happens to me, the guard has the chance to board the plane safely, without anyone being any wiser. This can also work out well, if I have some dodgy official, trying to arrest me! But they can't arrest me, if I don't have the money on me. There have been times, that I have wanted to tell them how stupid they were, as they missed the decoy! Our seats are booked together on the plane, and we usually have a laugh about those guys and then when the plane lands, I leave the airport and that's that!

Another security guard had a massive shock! This guy picked up a load of money from me and decided, in his wisdom, to strap the €5,000,000 in 500-euro notes, to his body, inside of his shirt. He was carrying an empty briefcase, in case someone tried to attack him and sure enough, he'd only gone about five hundred metres, when someone stunned him, with a Taser gun! With the impact of electricity to the back of his body, his legs gave way and he collapsed. The person who stole his briefcase, ran away meanwhile, some police officers saw the whole thing and went to assist my security guard. An ambulance arrived, to take him to the hospital and when they removed his shirt, they found the money, strapped to his body! The Police were involved and wanted to know why he was carrying five million euros? And why was he robbed?! The guard spoke with me and we provided proof of funds, but the corrupt police kept the cash, on a technicality!

When I was travelling through Vietnam, Cambodia and the Philippines, I saw more underground bunkers. These were different to the ones in Lansdowne, where I visited to install the cameras, for the exit and entry points, near Bath. These underground facilities contain billions and billions and billions, of US dollars and tonnes of Gold!

I have inspected 176 of them and they were all full.

I have only described what I have seen, in these three countries. Can you imagine, how many other underground bunkers there could possibly be, in the other 203 listed states around the world?! I am putting the reality of the greater picture, into perspective for you. Since Donald J Trump got into power, we have been asked not to move the money, as he knew it was there and it has now been taken over, by his elite team (The Kraken) and away from the CIA, who use it as drug money, for the Cabal.

Here's a tip for you.

If you are unsure about keeping your money in a bank and you want to know what other options there are for you, my current advice to people is to research, research and research some more! But it's good to know, there are choices out there. You can buy Gold, Silver or Platinum, as they will never lose their value. The Law tells you to declare it but it's not the Law. You have complete control over your personal wealth, possessions and data. It's about 'Free Will', as a human being.

Now then, if you are evil in nature, then naturally, you will only think of the negatives and do horrible things in your life, with other horrible people but the greater population is not evil. The majority of the world just want a good life for themselves, their loved ones and their future generations. To feel safe and secure, you have to take responsibility for yourself and learn as much as you can, as the more information you have, the more choices you can make. And if you get confused, by all of the information, then take a step back and speak to your God, speak to your Creator, speak to Allah or whomever you believe in and if you don't believe in anyone, then speak to your Mother or Grandmother and if that's not possible, find someone you trust and ask them.

When I feel like I need support in life or I would like some guidance, I speak to Lee because I know God is standing right by him and he can have a word with him, to see if he can help me out.

Private jet

$1,000,000

$100 bills, $100m per pallet

Gold

Gold Ingots

— CHAPTER 19 —
THE CHARLIE WARD SHOW

I started my YouTube channel ten years ago, which I used for fun! I would upload videos of happy times like Justin jumping into the swimming pool from the patio, our wedding and even a video of Nursel doing 'The Shiggy Challenge'!

I had 37 subscribers. As I enjoy going for walks along the beachfront and into the hills where I live, I thought to start recording these walks, to put on my channel. It was February 2020, when all of the headlines started spreading news that there was a deadly virus, which was going to affect the global population! Apparently, the first human cases of COVID-19, were identified in Wuhan, China, in December 2019. It was a week after this, which China confirmed, that human-to-human transmission of the virus, had taken place. Wuhan went into an unprecedented lockdown, on 23 January 2020 - at a time where the virus had killed 17 people and affected more than 400. The COVID-19 pandemic, also known as the coronavirus pandemic, is a contagious disease caused by severe acute respiratory syndrome, coronavirus 2. And so, the COVID-19 pandemic began and naturally, the public was scared!

But I knew it wasn't the truth!

I wanted to tell people that the virus was a smokescreen for the Global Financial Reset (GFR). "How do you know that, Charlie?!" You may ask. Because it has been verified by the people I have been talking to. "Who have you been talking to?" as you delve further. Carrying on reading and you will find out!

So, everyday I'd do a little update, to take people's fear away and I started to get some traction going, with additional subscribers and this told me that there are folks out there, who want to know more about what I have to say, with the current situation. I then started to end my videos by saying "Jesus loves you, but everyone else thinks you're a cunt!" It then became a catchphrase and my mate Alex loved it and he used the phrase regularly, when he went to the pub. It was catching on! But then someone said to me, that I may offend people, so I changed it "Jesus loves you, but everyone else thinks you're a twat!" Apparently this was more palatable!

The headlines continued around the world and all anybody could talk about was the virus that was baseless, but millions and millions of people were scared of it because the mainstream media had created a narrative. I talked often to my friend, Lee Dawson about the misinformation and I asked him, would he do a recorded Zoom call with me, just to explain more about the virus and the facts and how we should look after our health and our bodies. Lee is in the 'hall of fame' for one of the Mixed Martial Arts disciplines and he is also, very well known for training some of the top people in the world, in their disciplines. He is incredibly fit in health and supplies supplement products. So, I thought he was the perfect person, for sharing his wisdom and experiences, to the public.

When I started this journey, it was more educational, as I wanted people to do their own research. And when you start to do the research, you find it's nothing more than a common cold!

The coronavirus is a load of rubbish but let's learn something from this and educate ourselves.

You can't transmit a virus.

You can transmit a germ.

The human body is made up of viruses and it is fully equipped to kill an alien entity that enters its system. We call this the 'immune system' and you have to look after your immune system because it's the only one you've got!

One of my good friends, Steven Saunders, is a Michelin Star Chef and he suggested we could do a little video together, talking about healthy eating because if you look after your body, then your body will look after you. You don't need prescription drugs or vaccines, all you need is healthy food, exercise and love yourself, for who you are! So, we decided to set up this video in his kitchen and when he pressed record, he introduced me to The Charlie Ward Show, which I had never done previously. My channel only had my basic name, so I changed it, as I loved the title! I continued doing more videos and Lee said that we could get Dr. Sonia on the show because she knows about the current situation and she would be able to explain to people, what is going on as a doctor and a biologist, who is not paid by mainstream media or 'big pharma'.

More and more videos were going on the show and then Lee Hemington contacted me and said "I love what you're doing! I've set up an internet company at the start of lockdown and now everything, has come to a dead end and I don't know what to do, I could support you, promote you and do what I can to help you, get your message out to the people because I like what you're doing." I said "Yeh, that's great, we'll do that!" So, he was guiding me on social media because I hadn't got a clue! Suddenly, the numbers started going up in views and lots of new subscribers! Then my friend, Jack Kidd said "Well done, for sticking your neck out and telling the truth, I admire you!" Another friend, James Bland said "Well done!" A few young lads were very supportive of me, for standing out and telling people what was going on and there was Danny Robson saying to me "Well done for standing out and telling the truth!" It was amazing to hear! Also, Dorian Yates, the world famous body builder and Mr Olympia, six years in a row, thanked me for standing up for the truth.

Then one day, Jack told me about a guy, called Joseph Gregory Hallett, who was claiming to be the next King of England, 'King John III' and he asked if we could do a video, as a 'round table' on Zoom. "Yes!" I said "I have no idea who he is, I've never heard of him." This guy blew me away, as I had never even thought about challenging, the Royal Family. When we published the video, the numbers took off like a rocket! I was under 1,000 subscribers and this shot to 10,000, in no time at all! The interest in the new King, was massive! Then my friend, David Mahoney, who is a film producer and director approached me and said "This Joseph Gregory Hallett is fascinating to me and I would like to investigate it further. Can I take this story from you and do a documentary and a proper investigation?" I replied "Fine, he's done our show a lot of good, with boosting the numbers, so maybe, you should look at it."

My focus was getting the truth out there and getting people aware, that there is nothing to be scared of because there is a hidden agenda. The New World Order has been a long term plan and the deep state wants to distract you from the truth with vaccines, mask wearing, fear, riots, terrorist attacks, 5G, etc. I was determined to keep speaking, to as many people as I could, with different views and experiences, to give the audience the opportunity to do their own research.

YouTube congratulates you and gives you special awards, for different achievements. When you hit 100 subscribers, they let you have your own channel name, when you hit 1000, you get congratulations and so on. When you reach 100,000, you receive a special award…Nada! Nothing! Silence. They obviously did not think that I deserved that award? Or, was it something more sinister? I then started to notice, the numbers would go up and then back down again and one day, I was looking at the screen and in sixty seconds, I had lost 5,000 subscribers! I contacted YouTube and they said, it may be because people were unsubscribing but I knew the numbers were being tampered with and I carried on, as my intention was to keep going and getting the message out. The more people I interviewed, the more people wanted to tell me, about what they knew of the deep state and all of its evil, on humanity and folks were coming, from all over the world!

From the start of this journey, I have said "I have four corners of the puzzle and now I will find the rest of the puzzle, so when I get to the end, I'll have a clear picture of what I'm looking at. I found every single piece of that puzzle and on the journey, I also found some of the pieces were upside down. I also found some of the pieces that don't fit and it's been fascinating trying to put these pieces together and establish a clear picture of what's going on." So, when people say to me "Why should I trust your view?" I say "You don't have to. I'm asking you to do your own research, I've done over 3,000 hours of research and so has Lee Dawson and then we cross reference it." I cross reference my information, with six other people and before I put anything out to the public, I ensure the data is clear in truth and if I am unclear, then I don't put the video out. I have twenty five videos, that remain unpublished because I was asked not to share them with the public, by ex-CIA, ex-FBI, ex-Police, A-list actors and actresses, doctors and nurses, etc for various reasons, from a risk to their livelihoods and to some of them, their lives. "So, why did they contact you and do a video?" you may ask. They contacted me, to give me the facts, so I could share the truth with the public. These private conversations give me, their knowledge, wisdom and experiences, to share with others. Their identity is not important, it's the value of disclosing the truth and for me, to deliver it as accurately as possible, from our conversation together, to give to you.

176,000 subscribers, 300 videos and suddenly, YouTube took my channel down. They informed me that the reason for taking the channel down, because it was a 'scam' and 'fraud'! When I appealed against their decision, it got rejected in 12 seconds!!!

We then started all over again and built up our audience, to 60,000 and then that got taken down as well! And I went through the exact same procedure, I got the same response from them, I appealed and within seconds, they rejected it!

We built a third channel, I got to 15,000 subscribers and the same thing happened!

We built a fourth channel, reached 7,000 subscribers and the same thing happened!

As fast as we put them up, they got taken back down! It's like we were being watched...

Then one morning, when I came into the office and put my computer on, something had changed, it was different somehow as it was not how I left it, from the previous evening and I found out, that Google Chrome had managed to get into my computer and I could not log into my YouTube or Facebook accounts through Google Chrome, at all! They had contaminated my computer! The only way I could use social media was to use other website browsers, which allowed me to function. My Facebook account was 16 years old with hundreds of pictures and they told me that I did not follow the guidelines and broke their rules. I appealed to get my pictures back and they denied this, so in effect, they have stolen my pictures. That's theft! And you know, I do not respect thieves. Even my Instagram account got taken down and it won't allow me to go any further. I am not worried about any of this, as it simply exposes how desperate the Cabal wants to stop the truth from being revealed.

Once all of the platforms got taken down, Lee H. built up a great team of people behind the scenes and we built our own platform www.drcharlieward.com. Today is the last day of November 2020 and in just three weeks, we have had 60,000,000 views and currently have 3.5 million subscribers.

Recently, I said to my father "You always celebrate the death of Jesus because he died for your sins, I get that but the fact that you don't celebrate his birth, puts you on the fringe of Satanism, as you are celebrating death over life." He did not like those words that I put to him but I just came out with my truth.

It's a war between good and evil and it's not going to be easy!

Jesus Loves You

Charlie, Lee Dawson & Dorian Yates

David Mahoney, Jack Kidd, Charlie,
Lee Dawson, Justin and Corky

Steven Saunders.

Lee Hemmington

Lee Dawson

David Mahoney

Jack Kidd

Tara Dean

Mark Attwood

— AFTERWORD —
WHAT IS A CULT?

It is defined as some 'weird' religion that has rules, to be obeyed. The cult is completely convinced of its own righteousness and they believe you should obey the rules governed by them and that their 'faith' is the only faith to follow. And if you do not follow the rules, then you will be shamed into submission and you will fear what will happen to you because you broke the rules.

Now, I suggest you go and get a pen and some paper and write down what you think your government does for the people and its country? Write down how you think a bank looks after your money? Write down what you think any religion means to its followers? Write down what you think the police do for the communities? Write down what you think schools teach our children? And then look at it again and ask these questions to yourself?

Am I in a cult?

Do I believe that my church has the right rules?

Do I believe my government gives me rules?

Do I believe the police look after me?

Do I obey any of these corporations?

What will happen to me if I do not follow their rules?

Do I get shamed into submission?

Do I fear what will happen to me because I broke the rules?

And then, I will ask you again, are you in a cult?

I seek the truth, the whole truth and nothing but the truth.

2020 is deemed as 'The Great Awakening'. And going into 2021 and onwards, I will not hide the lies, which have existed in front of your eyes. It is going to be challenging, to see the truth exposed by the people you admired, believed in or placed on a pedestal but if you deny yourself this information, then it will be harder for you to get through it all. We are going into a New Age of Light (not New World Order) and you are part of it. Earth was a magical place before the darkness took over and turned us into their slaves. The devil has now lost its power and the light has won. We have new things to learn and old things to remember. But we must stand together and help one another to make a better world, for us all to live in harmoniously. This was not something that I planned, it's something that I have been led into. Thank you for all of your support, trust and love because without you, I wouldn't be here, sharing my life journey. Until we meet again, whether you watch one of my videos, to enjoy the company of the people I talk to. Or maybe, we'll have a glass of champagne, celebrating what a precious privilege it is, to be alive.

We are part of history, in the making and I wish to leave this world, in a better place, than I found it in, when I arrived on 8th June 1960.

Cheers!

IN MEMORY

OF

LEE RICHARD WARD

This is Justin, I hope you enjoyed my dads book,

Remember:

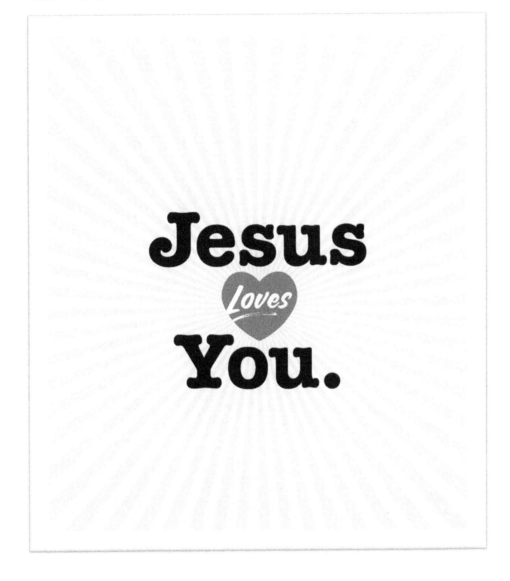

My foundations were unstable, from being a boy and turning into a man, where I threw myself into the unknown. I have dealt with every situation, with all that I knew...in that precise moment because, that was all I had and will ever have. We learn, evolve and every day, with each moment in time that we are here on this beautiful planet, we make choices, that can either enhance our experiences or not, whatever they may be.

I wish to give special thanks to everyone, that I have shared my life with because, I have my story to tell, in the only way I know how...with laughter, tears and craziness! Each and every one of you, has taught me different things, from the good to the bad and I am so grateful to you, thank you!

In no particular order:

Richard Norman Ward & Joan Mildred Ward. Benjamin James. Philippa Mildred. Priscilla Ruth. Rachel Pauline. Frank Ward. Norman Ward. Uncle Esmond. Uncle Frank Harvey Ward. Uncle Fergus. Mark Ward. Joan Puxdey. Jackson family. Mr.Proctor. Mick Mills, Trevor Whymark, Kevin Beattie, Arnold Muhren, Frans Thijssen and Bobby Robson. David Hemery Neil 'Tank' Prentice. Carl Jones. Janet Driver. Wendy and Carol Eton. Mrs Plumb. Veronica Mumford. Duke of Norfolk. Lance Clark. Arnold Ziff. Spencer Crookenden. William Barker and Eric Ward. Mrs Snuckowski. Lucy Labett. Sarah Labett. Paul Labett. Roger Labett. Mary Labett. Lois Leary. Alan Goody. Lee Richard Ward. Glenn Ward. Carla Jayne Ward. Hartley. Ray Lacy. Martin Nichols. Max. Graham Maynard. El Capistrano Beach Club. Roger Cook. Steve and Barry Parker. Stephen 'Stevie G' Grocutt. Simon Roach. Malky Mullen. Graham Maynard. Bird. Margaret and Denis Thatcher. Paul Shanks. Kenny Tokley. Terri La Conte. Russell Foster. Ged McGuirk, Nick Woodham, Norman Anderson and Matthew Evans. Soosie Dodd. Barry Hearn. Robert and Diane Atkin. Cliff & Barbara Thorburn. Willie & Fiona Thorne. The Chief of Police. Rachel

Baker. The Bush Tribes. Sol Kerzner. Barboza. Howard and Maureen Baker. Mr David Brown. Bob Dixon. Toby Neuth. Steve Hughes. James. Dawson Buck. Charlie & Ollie. Myra Hindley. Charles Bronson. Red Band. Paul Ambrose, Mark Johnson Allen, Ian Hutchinson, Richard Boot and Wayne Tatlock. Guy Kelland. Jim Davidson. Heather. Jane Ray. Suzy Ray. Sally Evans. Lee, Jeanine & Mia Clarson. Dominic Baldwin. . John, Teresa, Geoff, Chris and James Bracey. Ole Sigurdsson. Paul Duff, Roy Buck, Paul Porter and Dave Stronach. Sarah Wattam and Marcia McEwan. Max. Dwaine Hill. Prince of Johor Bahru. Miss Singapore. Reggie Wanchop, Steve Lever, Gary Morris and Kevin Lally. Dwaine. Brian Lunt. Thai Mafia. Freddie Foreman. Mel Williams. Bill Padley. Keith Floyd. Brian Lunt. Angela Meir. Philip Mason. Andy Quinton, Liam Ryan & Ingrid Katy DaSilva. Jesus Gill. Thierry Tissot. HH Prince Rashid. Rashid Al Habtoor. Joe McGrath. Sheikh Marwan & Sheikh Mohammed. Suhail Al Zarooni. Donald J Trump. King Juan Carlos. Adel Mardini. Ossama. Farooq. Mohammed. Gary Morris. Marie Fe Juliano. Edna. Robbie. Loopy loo. Nursel Akifova Feizulova. Justin. Ikbalya. Simon Bold. Desiree Florido. Luke and Caroline. Prince Rashid. Wendy Kidd. Jack Kidd. Debbie Parris. Astral Macalesher-Griffith. Joan. Cecily Spooner. Simon Giles. Stefan Booth. Linda & Dani Newman. Stuart & Vanessa Tidy. Benjamin & Tabitha. Harry. Sonni. Dennis. Sylvia. Gonzalo. Verity & Hugo. Henrietta & Baby Lee. Charlotte Nicholson. Pablo. Lee Dawson. Steven Saunders. Dr. Sonia. James Bland. Danny Robson. Dorian Yates. Joseph Gregory Hallett. David Mahoney. Lee Hemington. David Nino Rodriguez. Melody Krell. Tony Wilkinson. Mark Attwood. Danushia Kaczmarek.

Grateful Acknowledgement is made for the use of the following:

Wards of Stowmarket. Anglesea Road Hospital. Lucozade. Plymouth Brethren. Combs Ford Primary & Middle School. Bradleys. East Anglian Daily Times. Ipswich Town Football Club. Johnny Walker Red Label. Mexico Olympics, 1968. Health & Efficiency. Anglesea Road Hospital. Bear Inn Hotel. Clarks of Street & Clarks Shoes Head Office. Barkers of Earls Barton. Barrett shoes. "K" Shoes. Loakes. Ideal Home Exhibition London. Liverpool Street & Earl's Court Underground. Chorley Service Station. Fiat 500 variomatic. Peugeot 504. Welsh Male Voice Choir. The Island Bedding Centre. Godshill Church Cemetery. Isle of Wight County Press. St. Mary's Hospital Isle of Wight. Isle of Wight Ferry. Isle of Wight college of Arts and Technology. Amber Electrics. The Needles Isle of Wight. Facom. Snap On. Indian Restaurant in Sandown. South West Electric Board. The Boat Discotheque. Top Man. Hillesden Court, Grampian Court and Kingswear Park, Devon. Imperial Hotel, Torquay. Walton Hall. Warwickshire. The Cook Report. Wimbledon Village Report. Porsche 911. Child Support Agency (CSA). Torquay Magistrates Court. BoatHouse restaurant, Aston Martin Vantage Volante, Partners in Property from Sunderland. La Orquidea. Five Star Club. La Cartuja. Matchroom Country Club. Matchroom in England. Police Christmas Ball. Imperial House Tower. White Ladies Road. Monteith, Fairchild & Associates. Sondela Lodge. The River Club. The Wanderers Golf & Snooker Club. Mabula Lodge. The Hilton Garden Inn Hotel. Rolex. Ford Fiesta Escort and Sierra's. Virgin Atlantic Airlines. Royal Crescent Hotel, Bath. Camera. Sensormatic. HM Bristol Prison. HM Exeter Prison. HM Prison Dartmoor. Government Communications Headquarters (GCHQ). Military of Defence. HM Prison Whitemoor. HM Prison Cookham Wood. HM Prison Woodhill. HM Prison Dartmoor. HM Prison Swansea. HM Prison Gloucester. Honda Civic. David Lloyds Tennis Club. American Cruiser Rogue. Wedgies. MasterCraft. The Supercar Club, P1 International. Ferrari, Murcielago Lamborghini, McLaren, Aston Martin, Bentley. Vauxhall Cavalier. Miraflores. Max Beach Bar. Leisure Group Marketing. Ngee Ann City. Uber. Secret Service. Orchard Towers. Muddy Murphy's. The Legend. Clark Quay & Boat Quay. Sentosa Island. Bath University. Louis Vuitton, Coco Chanel, Gucci, Jimmy Choo. Absolute. Thai Mafia.

Eagles. Go Karting. Burasari Hotel. Floyd's Brasserie. Bangla Suites. Sea Pearl. Tsunami. Twin Sands Resort. Moët & Chandon. Tiananmen Square. Alternative Investment Market (AIM). South Beach Baptist Hospital. Harley Davidson. EagleRider. GWR Radio station. Quantum Financial System. GESARA & NESARA. The Grosvenor House Hotel. Federal Reserve. Antonev An-225. CIA. Criminal Investigation Departments (CID). Jetex. Customs. Phuket FantaSea Show. Pravda. Rolls Royce Phantom. Holder's House. Sandy Lane Hotel. Landmark Cottage. Harley Davidson-Fat Boy. Colonial House. Masquerade. The Green Monkey Bar. Portside. Tartrazine. Thomas Moor Boarding School. Bristol Football Club. Hercule CF Femerino, Sheffield Football Club. BUSA Team. Sheffield United Ladies. Birmingham City Women F.C. Spain's Got Talent. Nikki Beach. The Bank of Credit & Commerce International. Lloyds. HM Revenue & Customs (HMRC). The Kraken. YouTube. Mixed Martial Arts. David's Bar. London Pub. Mr Olympia. Royal Family & Queen. Google Chrome. Facebook. Instagram.

Photography Acknowledgments:

Underground Bunker:
somersetlive.co.uk - hidden-bunker-bath-corsham-war-4063672

Monkey Gland Sauce:
puddysoriginals.com

Rambo:
elephant-gin.com - elephant-gin-batch-rambo

Joseph Gregory Hallett:
kingjohnthethird.uk/photographs-of-greg/

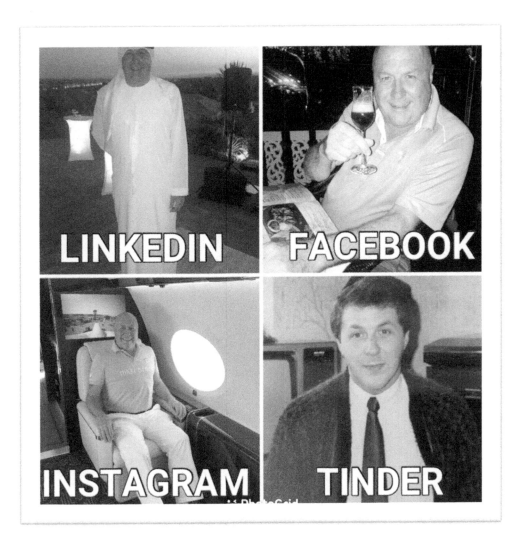

I'm, Just *Charlie*!

THE FOUR FACES OF CHARLIE WARD

www.DrCharlieWard.com

Made in the USA
Middletown, DE
04 May 2021